MW01616201

The Plutarch Project

Volume Eight

Marcus Brutus, Pericles, and Fabius

by

Anne E. White

The Plutarch Project Volume Eight: Marcus Brutus, Pericles, and Fabius
Copyright © 2020 by Anne E. White www.annewrites.ca

Cover photograph and design: Bryan White

All rights reserved. No part of this publication may be reproduced, stored in a retrieval system or transmitted in any form by any means, electronic, mechanical, photocopy, recording or otherwise, without the prior permission of the publisher, except as provided by Canadian copyright law.

ISBN: 978-1-7772522-2-9

CONTENTS

Introduction

A Dividing Line.—Both Shakespeare and Scott
use, as it were, a dividing line, putting on the one
side the wilful, wayward, the weak and the strong;
and on the other, persons who will. Faust, Lady
Macbeth, King Lear, Edward Waverley, Charles II.,
King John, Marlborough, all sorts of unlikely
persons, fall to the side of the line where Will is not
in command. On the other side, also, unlikely
people find themselves in company ...To make even
a suggestive list would be to range over all history
and literature. Let me say again, however, that here
is a line of study which should make our reading
profitable, as making us intimate with persons, and
the more able for life. (Charlotte Mason, *Ourselves*)

These notes, and the accompanying text, are prepared for the use of
individual students and small groups following a twelve-week term.
The text is that of Thomas North's 1579 translation of Plutarch's *Lives
of the Noble Greeks and Romans*, with substitutions from John Dryden's
1683 translation where it seemed useful.

In other volumes, I have used brackets to mark the changes from
North's translation; in this one, however, they have been omitted.
Please note that some omissions have **not** been noted. Those using
audio versions or other translations may therefore want to preview
those versions for suitability.

Each study contains explanatory material before the first lesson. A little
at the beginning may be useful to stir interest in the study, but it is not
meant to be given all in one dose!

Some lessons are divided into two or three sections. These can be read
all at once or used throughout the week.

I encourage you to make the lessons your own. Use the questions that are the most meaningful to you. Remember that Charlotte Mason was satisfied with "Proper names are written on the blackboard, and then the children narrate what they have listened to."

Examination Questions

The three studies include suggestions for end-of-term examinations. The questions for *Brutus* and *Pericles* were drawn from original P.N.E.U. programmes, and those for *Fabius* were written for this volume.

Marcus Brutus

(85-42 B.C.)

"But Brutus in contrary manner, for his virtue and valiantness, was well-beloved of the people and his own, esteemed of noble men...because he...had ever an upright mind with him..."

If you have read Plutarch's *Life of Publicola*, you will remember not only Lucius Junius Brutus (an ancestor of Marcus Brutus), but also the law made at the beginning of the Roman Republic, which said that it was permissible to take the life of anyone conspiring to seize the government and become a tyrant. In the story of Marcus Junius Brutus, that law was again put to the test.

Many students will have read one or more of the *Lives* corresponding to this time period, such as *Crassus, Julius Caesar, Pompey, Cato the Younger*, and *Cicero*; and will be familiar with events that took place during the life of Marcus Brutus. For those that have not, a short review is included.

Who was Marcus Junius Brutus?

Marcus Brutus, usually called Brutus, was born about the time that **Gaius Marius** was first elected consul of Rome. His father, also named Marcus Junius Brutus, was put to death in 77 B.C. (an act for which Pompey was blamed); so Brutus is sometimes referred to as Brutus the Younger.

The World of Marcus Brutus

Brutus grew up during a time of economic and military upheaval. Overseas conquests meant a great number of foreign captives; so small, family-run farms now competed with larger operations based on slave labour. The lack of small land owners forced the army to accept soldiers from the poorer classes, who then had to be paid more so that they could afford weapons. These soldiers considered themselves employees of the army (rather than citizens who occasionally had to fight): their loyalty was to their general, perhaps even more than to Rome itself.

Rome also became a dangerous place, as power shifted back and forth between Marius and his former lieutenant **Lucius Cornelius Sulla**, and as political "enemies" were repeatedly punished by **proscription**: confiscation of property and a death warrant, or exile if they could escape. (Those who have read Plutarch's *Life of Julius Caesar* will remember that Caesar, a nephew of Marius, spent time in hiding.)

The Government of the Roman Republic

The Roman Empire did not formally exist until Octavius Caesar (later Caesar Augustus) became Emperor in 27 B.C. However, though it was still the era of the **Roman Republic**, Rome did have an empire because of the large amount of foreign territory it had acquired. For clarity, we will call it the small-e **empire**.

Social Classes

There were two different types of class divisions in ancient Rome. The first was family-based, between the **patricians** (the nobility) and the

plebeians (common people). The second type were property- or wealth-based classes such as the *senatores*, who owned large amounts of land. The next level down, the **equestrian class** (in North's translation, the **knights of Rome**), was a "business class," made up of those who could afford horses and who therefore made up the cavalry in times of war. Besides the **equestrian** class, there were three lower classes of property owners; and, lowest of all, the **proletarii**.

Were the *senatores* the same as the senators?

Often, but the two were not identical. Over the centuries, and even within the Republic era, both the size of the Senate and the personal requirements for membership (age, wealth) changed. Some **plebeians** became senators along with the **patricians**. Those elected to **magistracies** (see below) were also included in the Senate.

What was an aedile, a quaestor, a consul?

The elected positions, or magistracies, in Rome were, starting at the bottom, quaestor, aedile, praetor, and consul. There were various numbers of each of these: for example, two consuls were elected each year. Ex-consuls could become censors; and a consul could become dictator if the need (usually a great emergency) arose.

What was the *praetor urbanis*?

The *praetor urbanis* was next in rank only to the consuls. He could summon the Senate or organize military defenses in their absence.

Who were the tribunes?

The duty of a non-military tribune (sometimes called a tribune of the plebeians, or plebs, or a tribune of the people) was to protect the common people from any individual or group (such as the nobles) who might suppress their rights. This position was not part of the junior-senior ranking of magistrates such as quaestor and consul; it was an office voted on by the common people (plebeians).

Can we integrate the reading with Shakespeare's *Julius Caesar*?

Shakespeare combined material from Plutarch's *Lives of Julius Caesar* and *Brutus* to write his version of the story. Notes on the play (Shakespeare Connections) are included in this study. If students have not already read *Julius Caesar*, you could make it the term's Shakespeare play; or you can simply refer to the relevant scenes.

Let's Talk Of Gaul, and Governors, and the other Brutus

Gaul, a Roman province inhabited by Celtic people, was divided into Transalpine Gaul ("Gaul-over-the-Alps"), covering parts of today's France, Belgium, and Germany; and Cisalpine Gaul ("Gaul-on-this-side-of-the-Alps"), today's Northern Italy. There are other, more correct names and divisions, but that is enough to read this *Life*.

Decimus Junius Brutus Albinus was the cousin of Marcus Brutus. Shakespeare misspells his name as Decius; and although he is part of the conspiracy (in the play), and goes to Caesar's house to escort him to the Senate, he doesn't do much that makes him memorable as a character. The real **Decimus Brutus** was a loyal supporter of Julius Caesar, a trusted friend who had fought with him in Gaul (in 58 B.C.), and even during his civil war; who nevertheless became annoyed with Caesar because he had not been given sufficient recognition for his loyalty and bravery. For example, he had expected a triumphal parade on his return from Gaul, but was denied it. However, Caesar seems to have been unaware of his resentment; his belief in Decimus' loyalty was key to the success of the conspiracy.

Decimus Brutus was acting governor of Transalpine Gaul from 48 to 46 B.C.; but Marcus Brutus, as Plutarch states, was governor of Cisalpine Gaul from 46 to 45 B.C. As we will read in **Lesson One**, Marcus Brutus had asked Caesar's pardon for fighting against him, and granting him that position shows that he had become a trusted friend. After the death of Caesar, Decimus Brutus was given the governorship of *Cisalpine* Gaul, and it was near the end of his term that he was besieged by Mark Antony (**Lesson Four**).

Decimus Brutus is always referred to as such in this story. "Brutus" refers to Marcus Brutus.

On the Map

Place names are listed under this heading. For consistency, I have used Dryden's spelling for places instead of North's. Charlotte Mason suggested using resources such as Dent's *Atlas of Ancient & Classical Geography*, which can be found online. A newer resource I have used myself is the *Historical Atlas of Ancient Rome* by Nick Constable (Checkmark Books/Thalamus Publishing, 2003).

Top Ten Vocabulary Terms in the *Life of Marcus Brutus*

If you recognize these words, you are well on your way to mastering the vocabulary for this *Life*. They will not be repeated in the lessons.

1. **choleric:** hot-tempered

2. **divers:** various, several

3. **factions:** groups divided by conflict or disagreement

4. **meet:** proper

5. **oration:** speech

6. **stay:** stop or delay

7. **tarry:** delay, wait; wait for someone or something

8. **tyrant:** a king or ruler who uses his power oppressively or unjustly

9. **victuals:** supplies, particularly food (pronounced *vittles*)

10. **word of the battle:** a pre-arranged signal to charge the enemy

Lesson One

Introduction

In 49 B.C., Julius Caesar crossed the border into Italy, along with his army, which was a deliberate act of defiance against Rome. After a short stop in the city of Rome to collect funds, and then a march into Spain to gather extra troops, he made his way to Greece, where, after a series of battles, he was finally declared the victor.

Brutus, at this time, was a younger man who had already earned respect in Rome both for his family connections and for his own honest nature. He was expected to take Caesar's side, largely because Pompey, who led the Roman defenses against Caesar, had been responsible for the death of Brutus' father when Brutus was still a child. However, this Brutus, like his ancestor, put loyalty to Rome ahead of personal animosities (or perhaps, as Plutarch suggests, there was another reason). In any case, he surprised Pompey by arriving at his camp to offer support.

Vocabulary

Capitol: the political and religious center of Rome, where the Temple of Jupiter and the **Forum** (see **Lesson Two**) were located. When the conspirators took refuge "in the Capitol" (**Lesson Two**), they barricaded themselves on the Capitoline Hill.

too hard a temper: To temper steel is to treat it so as to increase its strength. However, steel of too hard a temper breaks easily.

malice: hate

garboil: confusion

great battle…: the **Battle of Pharsalus**, see notes below

a breviary of Polybius: a history narration

would: wants; Dryden says "intends"

he begat him: he was his father

People

that **Junius Brutus:** see introductory notes for this study

Tarquins: the kings who ruled before the beginning of the Republic

Julius Caesar: Roman politician and general

Cassius: Gaius Cassius Longinus, Roman senator and general

Marcus Cato the philosopher: Marcus Porcius Cato Uticensis, the subject of the *Life of Cato the Younger*, an orator known for his moral integrity. Although he is called Cato the Younger, he had a son, also named Marcus Porcius Cato, mentioned in **Lesson Twelve.**

Ptolemy: Ptolemy of Cyprus, a king who committed suicide in 58 B.C. rather than submit to Roman power

Pompey: Gnaeus Pompeius Magnus, Roman statesman and general. He was defeated by Julius Caesar at the **Battle of Pharsalus.**

his father: Brutus the Elder; see introductory notes for this study

Historic Occasions

100 B.C.: birth of Julius Caesar

85 B.C.: birth of Brutus

49-45 B.C.: Civil war in Rome, called "Caesar's Civil War"; Brutus travelled to Greece to fight with Pompey against Caesar

48 B.C.: Battle of Pharsalus

46 B.C.: Battle of Thapsus (Caesar defeated loyalist forces including those led by Cato). Cato's death by suicide.

On the Map

Students should be given the opportunity to look at a map of the Roman Republic (or the Roman Empire) which shows Rome and its territories.

Places named in this lesson include **Cyprus**, the **Island of Rhodes, Pamphylia**, and **Cilicia**.

Reading

Part One

Marcus Brutus was descended from **that Junius Brutus** for whom the ancient Romans erected a statue of brass in the **Capitol** among the images of their kings with a drawn sword in his hand, because he had valiantly put down the **Tarquins** from their kingdom of Rome. But that Junius Brutus, being of a sour stern nature, not softened by reason, being like unto sword blades of **too hard a temper**, was so subject to his choler and the **malice** he bore unto the tyrants, that for their sakes he caused his own sons to be executed. But this Marcus Brutus in contrary manner, whose *Life* we presently write, having framed his manners of life by the rules of virtue and study of philosophy, and having employed his wit, which was gentle and constant, in attempting of great things, seems to have been of a temper exactly framed for virtue. So that his very enemies which wish him most hurt, because of his conspiracy against **Julius Caesar**; if there were any noble attempt done in all this conspiracy, they refer it wholly unto Brutus, and all the cruel and violent acts unto **Cassius**, who was Brutus' familiar friend, but not his equal in honesty and pureness of purpose.

[omission for length]

Part Two

Marcus Cato the philosopher was brother unto Servilia, Marcus Brutus' mother: and he it was whom Brutus studied most to follow of all the other Romans, because he was his uncle; and (after Cato's death) he married his daughter Porcia.

[omission for length]

When he was but a very young man, he accompanied his uncle Cato

8

to **Cyprus**, when he was sent there against **Ptolemy**. But when Ptolemy killed himself, Cato, being by some necessary business detained in the **Island of Rhodes**, had already sent Canidius, one of his friends before, to keep the king's treasure and goods. But Cato, fearing he would be light-fingered, wrote unto Brutus forthwith to come out of **Pamphylia** (where he was but newly recovered of a sickness) into Cyprus, the which he did. The which journey he was sorry to take upon him, both for respect of Canidius' shame, whom Cato as he thought wrongfully slandered, as also because he thought this office too mean and unmeet for him, being a young man, and given to his book. This notwithstanding, he behaved himself so honestly and carefully that Cato did greatly commend him; and after all the goods were sold and converted into ready money, he took the most part of it, and returned withal to Rome.

Part Three

Afterwards when the empire of Rome was divided into factions, and that Caesar and **Pompey** both were in arms one against the other, and that all the empire of Rome was in **garboil** and uproar: it was thought then that Brutus would take part with Caesar, because Pompey not long before had put **his father** unto death. But Brutus, preferring the respect of his country and commonwealth before private affection, and persuading himself that Pompey had juster cause to enter into arms than Caesar, he then took part with Pompey, though oftentimes meeting him before he thought scorn to speak to him, thinking it a great sin and offence in him to speak to the murderer of his father. But now, looking upon him as the general of his country, he placed himself under his command, and set sail for **Cilicia**, to be lieutenant to Sestius, who had the government of that province.

But when he saw that there was no way to rise, nor to do any noble exploits, and that Caesar and Pompey were both camped together, and fought for victory: he went of himself unsent for into Macedon to be partaker of the danger. It is reported that Pompey being glad, and wondering at his coming, when he saw him come to him, he rose out of his chair, and went and embraced him before them all, and used him as honourably as he could have done the noblest man that took his part.

Brutus, being in Pompey's camp, did nothing but study all day long, except while he was with Pompey; and not only the days before, but the selfsame day also before the **great battle was fought in the fields of Pharsalus**, where Pompey was overthrown. It was in the midst of summer, and the sun was very hot, besides that the camp was lodged near unto marshes, and they that carried his tent tarried long before they came, whereupon, being very weary with travel, scant any meat came into his mouth at dinner time. Furthermore, when others slept, or thought what would happen the morrow after, he fell to his book, and wrote all day long till night, writing **a breviary of Polybius**.

It is said that Caesar had so great a regard for him that he ordered his commanders by no means to kill Brutus in the battle, but to spare him if possible, and to bring him safe to him, if he would willingly surrender himself; but if he made any resistance, to suffer him to escape rather than do him any violence. Some say he did this for Servilia's sake, Brutus' mother. For, when he was a young man, he had been acquainted with Servilia, who was extremely in love with him. And because Brutus was born in that time, he persuaded himself that **he begat him**.

[omission for content]

So, after Pompey's overthrow at the **Battle of Pharsalus**, when Caesar came to besiege his camp, Brutus went out of the camp gates unseen of any man, and leapt into a marsh full of water and reeds. Then when night was come he crept out, and went unto the city of Larissa: from whence he wrote unto Caesar, who was very glad that he had escaped, and sent for him to come unto him. When Brutus was come, he did not only pardon him, but also kept him always about him, and did as much honour and esteem him as any man he had in his company.

[omission for length]

Brutus in the meantime gained Caesar's forgiveness for his friend Cassius; and pleading also in defense of the king of the Libyans, though he was overwhelmed with the greatness of the crimes alleged against him, yet by his entreaties and deprecations to Caesar in his behalf, he preserved to him a great part of his kingdom. They say also that Caesar said, when he heard Brutus plead: "I know not," said he, "what this young man **would**, but, whatever he **would**, he willeth it vehemently." For Brutus' gravity and constant mind would not grant all men their requests that sued unto him; but being moved with reason and discretion, he did always incline to that which was good and honest.

[omission for length]

Narration and Discussion

What was Brutus like as a young man? Why did he decide to support Pompey in the civil war?

Plutarch says that "Brutus' gravity and constant mind would not grant all men their requests that sued unto him." Why is it sometimes better not to agree to everything asked of us?

Creative Narration: In Dryden's words: "From Larissa he wrote to Caesar who expressed a great deal of joy to hear that he was safe, and, bidding him come, not only forgave him freely, but honoured and esteemed him among his chiefest friends." Taking the role of Julius Caesar, start a list of "Reasons I Like Brutus." Continue adding to the list during the next lesson. You might decide to add a second list, "Reasons I Am Not Sure Brutus Likes Me."

Creative Narration for older students: Divide a sheet of paper in two, and list similarities and contrasts between Brutus and Cassius.

Lesson Two

Introduction

Part One: Brutus appreciated the benefits of Caesar's friendship.
Part Two: Brutus helped to plan Caesar's assassination.
How did one follow so closely on the other?

Shakespeare Connections

The conspiracy and the assassination of Julius Caesar are dramatized in Act 1, Act 2, and Act 3, Scene 1.

Plutarch writes of Caesar: "'It is not,' said he, 'the fat and the long-haired men that I fear, but the pale and the lean,' meaning Brutus and Cassius." In Act 1, Scene 2, Shakespeare writes "Let me have men about me that are fat, / Sleek-headed men and such as sleep a-nights. / Yond Cassius has a lean and hungry look, / He thinks too much; such men are dangerous." Plutarch includes Brutus as the target of Caesar's comment, but Shakespeare does not; do you think there was a reason for that?

A small point of character interest occurs in Act 1, Scene 2, where Shakespeare drops the name of Titinius into a speech, establishing a connection between him and Julius Caesar. In Plutarch's narrative, Titinius is introduced much later and said to be a friend of Cassius. The brief line here functions as the first mention of a character who will be used later on.

Vocabulary

a great good hap: very fortunate

praetorship of the city; the first praetorship: *praetor urbanis*; see introductory notes

contention: something being argued over or fought for (as in the phrase "bone of contention").

listed: wished, chose

vigour of purpose: power to act; will

rancour: anger, resentment

estimation: high esteem, having a good reputation

grew strange together: had not much to do with each other

People

Scipio: Quintus Caecilius Metellus Scipio; governor of Syria; father-in-law of Pompey; fought at the Battle of Thapsus

Antony: Marcus Antonius, usually called Mark Antony or Antony in English; a Roman general and politician, supporter of Caesar; later part of the Second Triumvirate.

Dolabella: Publius Cornelius Dolabella, a Roman general and politician

Tillius Cimber: Shakespeare calls him Metellus Cimber.

Casca: Publius Servilius Casca Longus, one of the conspirators

Historic Occasions

March 44 B.C.: Death of Julius Caesar

On the Map

Africa: The Roman province called Africa

Gaul in Italy: Cisalpine Gaul; see introductory notes for this study

Parthia: a kingdom in the Middle East

Megara: a city and region in Attica. There will be more details about Megara later on.

Reading

Part One

Now when Caesar took sea to go into **Africa** against Cato and **Scipio**, he left Brutus as governor of Gaul in Italy, on this side of the Alps, which was **a great good hap** for that province. For while people in other provinces were in distress with the violence and greed of their governors, and suffered as much oppression as if they had been slaves and captives of war, Brutus, by his easy government, made them amends for their calamities under former rulers, directing moreover all their gratitude for his good deeds to Caesar himself. For when Caesar returned out of Africa, and progressed up and down Italy, the things that pleased him best to see were the cities under Brutus' charge and government, and Brutus himself: who honoured Caesar in person, and whose company also Caesar greatly esteemed.

Now several praetorships being vacant, it was looked for that Brutus or Cassius would make suit for the chiefest praetorship, which they called the **praetorship of the city**: because he that had that office was as a judge to minister justice unto the citizens. Therefore they strove one against the other, though some say that there was some little grudge betwixt them for other matters before, and that this **contention** did set them further out, though they were allied together. For Cassius had married Junia, Brutus' sister. Others say, that this contention betwixt them came by Caesar himself, who secretly gave either of them both hope of his favour. This provoked them at last to an open competition and trial of their interests. Brutus had only the reputation of his honour and virtue to oppose to the many and gallant actions performed by Cassius against the **Parthians**. So Caesar, after he had heard both their objections, told his friends with whom he consulted about this matter: "Cassius' cause is the juster," said he, "but Brutus must be first preferred." Thus Brutus had the **first praetorship**, and Cassius the second: who thanked Caesar not so much for the praetorship he had, as he was angry with him for that which he had lost.

But Brutus in many other things tasted of the benefit of Caesar's favour in anything he requested. For, if he had **listed**, he might have been one of Caesar's chiefest friends, and of greatest authority and credit about him. Howbeit Cassius' friends did dissuade him from it, (for Cassius and he were not yet reconciled together since their first contention and strife for the praetorship); and they prayed him to beware of Caesar's sweet enticements, and to fly his tyrannical favours: the which they said Caesar gave him not to honour his virtue, but to unbend his strength, and undermine his **vigour of purpose**.

Now Caesar on the other side did not trust him overmuch, nor was Brutus not without tales brought unto him against him: howbeit he feared his great mind, authority, and friends. Yet, on the other side also, he trusted his good nature and fair conditions. When it was told him that **Antony** and **Dolabella** designed some disturbance, "It is not," said he, "the fat and the long-haired men that I fear, but the pale and the lean," meaning Brutus and Cassius. At another time also, when one accused Brutus unto him, and bade him beware of him: "What," said he again, clapping his hand on his breast, "think ye that Brutus will not tarry till this body die?" Meaning that none but Brutus, after him, was meet to have such power as he had. And surely, in my opinion, I am persuaded that Brutus might indeed have come to have been the chiefest man of Rome, if he could have contented himself for a time to have been next unto Caesar, and to have suffered his glory and authority which he had gotten by his great victories to consume with time.

But Cassius being a choleric man, and hating Caesar privately more than he did the tyranny openly, he incensed Brutus against him. Brutus felt the rule an oppression, but Cassius hated the ruler; and, among other reasons on which he grounded his quarrel against Caesar, the loss of his lions (which he had procured when he was aedile-elect) was one; for Caesar, finding these in **Megara**, when that city was taken by Calenus, seized them to himself.

[*omission for length: examples of Cassius' hot temper*]

Now when Cassius felt his friends, and did stir them up against Caesar, they all agreed and promised to take part with him, so long as Brutus were the chief of their conspiracy. For they told him that so high an enterprise and attempt as that did not so much require men of manhood and courage to draw their swords, as it stood them upon to have a man of such **estimation** as Brutus, to make every man boldly think that by his only presence the fact were holy and just. If he took not this course, then that they should go to it with fainter hearts, and when they had done it they should be more fearful: because every man would think that Brutus would not have refused to have made one with them, if the cause had been good and honest. Therefore Cassius, considering this matter with himself, did first of all speak to Brutus since **they grew strange together** for the suit they had for the praetorship. So when he was reconciled to him again, and that that they had embraced one another, Cassius asked him if he were determined to be in the Senate-house, the first day of the month of March, because he heard say that Caesar's friends should move the council that day, that Caesar should be called "King" by the Senate. Brutus answered him he would not be there. "But if we be sent for," said Cassius, "how then?" "For myself then," said Brutus, "I mean not to hold my peace, but to withstand it, and rather die than lose my liberty."

[Omission for length and content: Brutus and Cassius began to gather men "whom they thought stout enough to attempt any desperate matter." Some of their recruits were said to have joined only because Brutus was involved. Brutus spent many sleepless nights worrying about the plan, and his wife was greatly concerned.]

Part Two

[Omission for length: Caesar's somewhat delayed arrival at Pompey's Theatre, on the Ides of March]

When Caesar was come into the house, all the senate rose to honour him at his coming in. So when he was set, the conspirators flocked about him, and amongst them they presented one **Tillius Cimber**, who pleaded humbly for the calling home again of his brother that was banished. They all made as though they were intercessors for him, and took him by the hands and kissed him. Caesar at the first simply refused their kindness and entreaties: but afterwards, perceiving they still pressed on him, he violently thrust them from him. Then Cimber, with both his hands, plucked Caesar's gown over his shoulders; and **Casca**, that stood behind him, drew his dagger first, and strake Caesar upon the shoulder, but gave him no great wound. Caesar, feeling himself hurt, took him straight by the hand he held his dagger in, and cried out in Latin: "O traitor Casca, what doest thou?" Casca, on the other side cried in Greek, and called his brother to help him. So several people running on a heap together to fly upon Caesar, he looking about him to have fled, saw Brutus with a sword drawn in his hand ready to strike at him: then he let Casca's hand go, and, casting his gown over his face, suffered every man to strike at him that would.

Then the conspirators thronging one upon another, because every man was desirous to have a cut at him, so many swords and daggers lighting upon one body, one of them hurt another, and among them Brutus caught a blow on his hand, because he would make one in murdering of him; and all the rest also were every man of them bloodied.

Part Three

Caesar being slain in this manner, Brutus, standing in the midst of the house, would have spoken, and stayed the other senators that were not of the conspiracy, to have told them the reason why they had done this fact. But they, as men both afraid and amazed, fled one upon another's neck in haste to get out at the door, and no man followed them. For it was set down and agreed between them that they should kill no man but Caesar only, and should entreat all the rest to look to defend their liberty. All the conspirators but Brutus, determining upon this matter, thought it good also to kill Antony, because he was a wicked man, and that in nature favoured tyranny: besides also, for that he was in great estimation with soldiers, having been conversant of long time amongst them: and specially having a mind bent to great enterprises, he was also of great authority at that time, being consul with Caesar.

But Brutus would not agree to it. First, for that he said it was not honest: secondly, because he told them there was hope of change in him. For he did not mistrust, but that Antony, being a noble-minded and courageous man, (when he should know that Caesar was dead) would willingly help his country to recover her liberty, having them an example unto him, to follow their courage and virtue. So Brutus by this means saved Antony's life, who at that present time disguised himself and stole away.

Narration and Discussion

How did Julius Caesar's respect help move Brutus up the ladder in Rome?

How did Brutus come to believe that he was doing an honourable act by conspiring to kill Caesar?

For older students: In Dante's *Inferno*, three unfaithful servants are pictured being eaten by Satan's three mouths: Brutus, Cassius, and Judas Iscariot. Do you agree with such a judgment on Brutus?

For older students: "… the which they said Caesar gave him not to honour his virtue, but to unbend his strength, and undermine his vigour of purpose." The issue of power and its misuses is a very large one. Write about or discuss examples of "sweet enticements," or those which, though seemingly well meant, may stunt one's "vigour of purpose," or Will (as Charlotte Mason put it).

> "...though we are slow to elect for ourselves, we are
> zealous propagandists on behalf of others.
> We...push them zealously into that which we are
> assured is for their good... but, in so far as we have
> chosen for another, we have done that other person
> an injury..." (Charlotte Mason, *Ourselves*)

Creative Narration #1: This reading offers several possible subjects for drawing or painting. Can you find any paintings that were inspired by this story?

Creative Narration #2: See previous lesson.

Lesson Three

Introduction

Julius Caesar was dead, and there were many questions in the air. What would happen to Rome now? What would the consequences be for Brutus and the other conspirators? Would Brutus' reputation save him from the vengeance of those who supported Caesar?

Shakespeare Connections

"Afterwards, when Caesar's body was brought into the marketplace, Antony making his funeral oration in praise of the dead...taking Caesar's gown all bloody in his hand, he laid it open to the sight of them all, shewing what a number of cuts and holes it had upon it." Act 3, Scene 2 contains Antony's funeral oration, and the reaction of the

Roman people to his words.

"And because someone called him by his name, Cinna, the people thinking he had been that Cinna who in an oration he made had spoken very evil of Caesar, they falling upon him in their rage slew him outright in the marketplace." This event takes place in Act 3, Scene 3.

Vocabulary

marketplace: the Forum in Rome, a central area between the government buildings, where speeches were made, public ceremonies were conducted, etc.

pulpit for orations: the place from which speeches were made

returned again into the Capitol: they were using the Capitol as a refuge until they could be assured of their own safety

stayed and quenched: prevented

governments of provinces: It is important to note that these governorships were not to take effect until the following January.

in hugger mugger: quietly, in secret

marred all: caused trouble, ruined everything

People

Cinna, #1 and #2: This involves a case of mistaken identity.

Cicero: Marcus Tullius Cicero, the subject of Plutarch's *Life of Cicero*

Lepidus: Marcus Aemilius Lepidus, Roman general and statesman; consul in 46 and 42 B.C.; supporter of Julius Caesar. He became one of the Second Triumvirate in October 43 B.C.

Decimus (Junius) Brutus Albinus: Roman general and a cousin of Marcus Brutus. Please read the introductory notes for this study.

Trebonius: one of the conspirators, who was later killed by Dolabella

On the Map

Several Roman provinces are named in this lesson, such as **Crete**;
Africa; **Asia**; **Bithynia**; **Cisalpine Gaul**. Note that **Asia** did not
refer to the whole continent, but to the area that had been the
Kingdom of Lydia, the northwestern part of present-day Turkey.
Likewise, **Africa** included only parts of northern Africa.

Reading

Part One

But Brutus and his party, having their swords bloody in their hands,
went straight to the Capitol, persuading the Romans as they went to
take their liberty again. Now, at the first time when the murder was
newly done, there were sudden outcries of people that ran up and
down the city, the which indeed did the more increase the fear and
tumult. But when they saw they slew no man, neither did spoil or make
havoc of anything, then certain of the senators and many of the people,
emboldening themselves, went to the Capitol unto them.

There a great number of men being assembled together one after
another, Brutus made an oration unto them to win the favour of the
people, and to justify that they had done. All those that were by said
they had done well, and cried unto them that they should boldly come
down from the Capitol. Whereupon, Brutus and his companions came
boldly down into the **marketplace**. The rest followed in troop, but
Brutus went foremost, very honourably compassed in round about
with the noblest men of the city, which brought him from the Capitol,
through the marketplace, to the **pulpit for orations**.

At the sight of Brutus, the crowd, though consisting of a confused
mixture and all disposed to make a tumult, were struck with reverence,
and awaited what he would say with order and with silence. When
Brutus began to speak, they gave him quiet audience: howbeit
immediately after, they shewed that they were not all contented with
the murder. For when **Cinna** would have spoken, and began to accuse
Caesar, they fell into a great uproar among them, and marvellously
reviled him; insomuch that the conspirators **returned again into the
Capitol**. There Brutus, being afraid to be besieged, sent back again the

noblemen that came thither with him, thinking it no reason that they, which were no partakers of the murder, should be partakers of the danger.

Then the next morning the Senate being assembled, and Antony, Plancus, and **Cicero** having made a motion that they should take an order to pardon and forget all that was past, and to establish friendship and peace again: it was decreed, that they should not only be pardoned, but also that the consuls should refer it to the Senate what honours should be appointed unto them. This being agreed upon, the Senate broke up, and Antony, to put them in heart that were in the Capitol, sent them his son for a pledge. Upon this assurance, Brutus and his companions came down from the Capitol, where every man saluted and embraced each other; among the which, Antony himself did bid Cassius to supper to him; and **Lepidus** also bade Brutus; and so one bade another, as they had friendship and acquaintance together.

Part Two

The next day following, the Senate, being called again to council, did first of all commend Antony, for that he had wisely **stayed and quenched** the beginning of a civil war; then they also gave Brutus and his consorts great praises; and lastly they appointed them several **governments of provinces**. For unto Brutus, they appointed **Crete**; **Africa**, unto Cassius; **Asia**, unto **Trebonius**; **Bithynia**, unto Cimber; and unto **Decimus Brutus Albinus**, Gaul on this side the Alps.

When this was done, they came to talk of Caesar's will and testament, and of his funerals and tomb. Then Antony thinking good his testament should be read openly, and also that his body should be honourably buried, and not **in hugger mugger**, lest the people might thereby take occasion to be worse offended if they did otherwise, Cassius stoutly spoke against it. But Brutus went with the motion, and agreed unto it: wherein it seemeth he committed a second fault. For the first fault he did was when he would not consent to his fellow conspirators' proposal that Antony should be slain: and therefore he was justly accused, that thereby he had saved and strengthened a strong and grievous enemy of their conspiracy. The second fault was when he agreed that Caesar's funerals should be as Antony would have them: the which indeed **marred all**. For first of all, when Caesar's testament was openly read among them, whereby it appeared that he bequeathed unto every citizen of Rome seventy-five drachmas a man; and that he left his gardens and arbours unto the people, which he had on this side of the Tiber River, in the place where now the Temple of Fortune is built. The people then loved him, and were marvellous sorry for him.

Afterwards, when Caesar's body was brought into the marketplace, Antony making his funeral oration in praise of the dead, according to the ancient custom of Rome, and perceiving that his words moved the common people to compassion: he framed his eloquence to make their hearts yearn the more, and, taking Caesar's gown all bloody in his hand, he laid it open to the sight of them all, shewing what a number of cuts and holes it had upon it.

Therewithal the people fell presently into such a rage and mutiny, that there was no more order kept amongst the common people. For some of them cried out, "Kill the murderers"; others plucked up benches and tables out of the shops round about; and having laid them all on a heap together, they set them on fire, and thereupon did put the body of Caesar, and burnt it in the midst of the most holy places. And furthermore, when the fire was thoroughly kindled, some here, some there, took burning firebrands, and ran with them to the murderers' houses that had killed him, to set them afire. Howbeit the conspirators, foreseeing the danger before, had wisely provided for themselves, and fled.

But there was a poet called **Cinna**, who had been no partaker of the conspiracy, but was always one of Caesar's chiefest friends. This man dreamed that he was invited to supper by Caesar, and that he declined to go, but that Caesar entreated and pressed him to it, very earnestly; and at last, taking him by the hand, led him into a very deep and dark place, whither he was forced against his will to follow in great consternation and amazement. This dream put him all night into a fever, and yet notwithstanding, the next morning when he heard that they carried Caesar's body to burial, being ashamed not to accompany his funerals: he went out of his house, and thrust himself into the press of the common people that were in a great uproar. And because someone called him by his name, Cinna, the people thinking he had been that Cinna who in an oration he made had spoken very evil of Caesar, they falling upon him in their rage slew him outright in the marketplace.

[omission for length. The conspirators fled the city in fear, which allowed Mark Antony to take control. He was not popular with the common people, and the feeling among them was a wish for Brutus' presence, especially at the games in honour of Apollo. However, Rome still seemed too dangerous a place for Brutus.]

Narration and Discussion

Do you think Brutus was as hard-hearted as his ancestor Brutus (mentioned in **Lesson One**)? Or was he not cruel enough (should he have agreed to kill Antony as well)? What might happen because of that decision?

For older students: Charlotte Mason wrote:

> "Several times a day we shall find two ideas
> presented to our minds; and we must make our
> choice upon right and reasonable grounds. The
> things themselves which stand for the ideas may not
> seem to matter much; but the choice matters. Every
> such exercise makes personality the stronger; while
> it grows the weaker for every choice we shirk."

She also said:

> "These foreign ideas get in with a rush. We know
> how that just man, Othello, was instantly
> submerged by the idea of jealousy which Iago
> cunningly presented." (Charlotte Mason, *Ourselves*)

So far we have seen both Cassius and Antony use the power of small ideas to turn others to their way of thinking. How can we guard against being swayed to make unwise or immoral choices?

Lesson Four

Introduction

The time period covered by this lesson spans the summer of 44 B.C., through the rest of that year and the early winter of the next. The events of those months could fill a long list of Historic Occasions. First was the post-assassination arrival and rising popularity of young Octavius, Caesar's heir. Then in December of 44 B.C., Mark Antony began a civil war by besieging Decimus Brutus (see **Lesson Three**), the outgoing governor of Cisalpine Gaul, in the city of Mutina (present-day Modena, in Northern Italy).

The senate, at their meeting in January of 43 B.C., was divided: some wanted to negotiate with Antony, others (such as Cicero) believed that only strong military action would stop him. Another strategy proposed at this time was that all new governorships (which traditionally started in January) should be cancelled, and those who currently held those positions should continue in them for another year. This act would allow Decimus Brutus to remain governor of Gaul; otherwise he might become the outlaw in a standoff with Roman authorities, rather than the other way around.

While all this was happening in Italy, Marcus Brutus was seemingly enjoying philosophical studies in Greece; but he was also gathering an army to fight for his beloved Roman Republic. He began capturing cities and whole territories, to keep them safe (so to speak) against potential tyrants. At the beginning of 43 B.C., he was able to write to the Senate that he was in command of Macedon, Illyricum, and Greece. However, the situation with Antony was quickly growing worse, and that commanded most of the Romans' attention.

Vocabulary

curry favour: do nice things to make people like you

mild and courteous bondage: slavery, but nice slavery

usurped tyranny: unlawful tyranny, vs., perhaps, upright tyranny

Hector parting from Andromache: in *The Iliad*, the scene where Hector says goodbye to his wife and young son

People

Octavius Caesar: Gaius Octavius, or Octavius; later called Caesar

Augustus; who became the first Roman Emperor in 27 B.C. At the beginning of 43 B.C., he was made *propraetor* and given command of troops, although he was not yet twenty years old. **Note on translations of his name:** North uses "Octavius Caesar." Dryden refers to him as "Young Caesar" or, later, just "Caesar." Other books, such as Genevieve Foster's *Augustus Caesar's World*, say "Octavian." For consistency in these notes, I have used "Octavius."

the captain of those ships: seemingly his friend Marcus Appuleius

prognostication: prediction

Leto's son: the Greek god Apollo

Gaius (Antony's brother), or **Gaius Antonius:** He was *praetor urbanis* in 44 B.C., while his older brother Mark Antony was consul and a third brother, Lucius Antony, was a tribune. After Caesar's assassination, he was appointed governor of Macedonia, which is why he was traveling there at that time.

Gabinius: Aulus Gabinius, a "tribune of the people"

Cicero's son: Cicero the Younger, born in 65 B.C. **Trivia:** another young soldier recruited by Brutus at this time was Quintus Horatius Flaccus, later known as the poet Horace.

Historic Occasions

August 44 B.C.: Brutus sailed to Greece

December 44 B.C.: Conflict between Decimus Brutus and Antony, the outgoing and incoming governors of Cisalpine Gaul

January 43 B.C.: Aulus Hirtius and Gaius Vibius Pansa took office as consuls

Winter 43 B.C.: Brutus fell ill at Dyrrhachium, but recovered and began capturing cities "for the Republic."

On the Map

Apollonia: A city founded by the Greeks, in the region called Illyria; home to a school of philosophy during the Roman era; it was taken by Brutus for Pompey during the war against Caesar. Its ruins are located in present-day Albania.

through the country of Lucania unto the city of Elea: Elea, also called Velia, was a city on the coast of the Tyrrhenian Sea.

Athens: a city-state in Greece (now the capital city)

Macedon: or Macedonia; the kingdom to the north of Greece

Carystus: or Karistos, a town on the island of **Euboea** (sometimes called Chalcis), which is the second-largest Greek island after Crete

Dyrrhachium: a city now called Durrës, in Albania

Reading

Part One

Now the state of Rome standing in these terms, there fell out another change and alteration, when the young man **Octavius Caesar** came to Rome. He was the son of Julius Caesar's niece, whom he had adopted for his son and made his heir by his last will and testament. But when Julius Caesar, his adopted father, was slain, he was in the city of **Apollonia** where he studied, and where he was expecting also to meet Caesar on his way to the expedition which he had determined on against the Parthians; but when he heard the news of his death, he returned again to Rome, where to begin to **curry favour** with the common people. He first of all took upon him his adopted father's name, and made distribution among them of the money which his father had bequeathed unto them. By this means he troubled Antony sorely; and by force of money got a great number of his father's soldiers together, that had served in the wars with him.

And Cicero himself, for the great malice he bare Antony, sided with young Caesar. But (Marcus) Brutus marvellously reproved Cicero for it, and wrote unto him, that he seemed by his doings not to be sorry to have a master, but only to be afraid to have one that should hate him: and that all his doings in the commonwealth did witness that he chose to be subject to a **mild and courteous bondage**, since by his words and writings he did commend this young man Octavius Caesar to be a good and gentle lord. "For our predecessors," said he, "would never abide to be subject to any masters, how gentle or mild soever they were"; and, for his own part, that he had never resolutely determined with himself to make war, or peace, but otherwise, that he was certainly minded never to be slave nor subject. And therefore he wondered much at him, how Cicero could be afraid of the danger of civil wars, and would not be afraid of a shameful peace; and that to thrust Antony out of the **usurped tyranny**, in recompense he Cicero went about to establish young Octavius Caesar as tyrant. These were the contents of Brutus' first letters he wrote unto Cicero.

Now, the city of Rome being divided in two factions, some taking part with Antony, other also leaning unto Octavius Caesar, and the soldiers selling themselves, as it were, by public outcry, and going over to whoever would give them most: Brutus, seeing the state of Rome would be utterly overthrown, therefore determined to go out of Italy, and went afoot **through the country of Lucania unto the city of Elea**, by the seaside. There Porcia, being ready to depart from her husband Brutus and to return to Rome, did what she could to dissemble the grief and sorrow she felt at her heart: but, in spite of all her constancy, a picture which she found there accidentally betrayed it. It was a Greek subject, **Hector parting from Andromache** when he went to engage the Greeks, giving his young son Astyanax into her arms, and she fixing her eyes upon him. When she looked at this piece, the resemblance it bore to her own condition made her burst into tears, and several times a day she went to see the picture, and wept before it.

[omission for length]

Part Two

(Marcus) Brutus took ship from thence, and sailed to **Athens**, where he was received by the people with great demonstration of kindness, expressed in their acclamation and the honours that were decreed him. He lived there with a friend of his, with whom he went daily to hear the lectures of Theomnestus, an Academic philosopher, and of Cratippus the Peripatetic, and so would talk with them in philosophy, that it seemed he left all other matters, and gave himself only unto study: howbeit secretly, notwithstanding, he made preparation for war.

For he sent one of his captains, Herostratus, into **Macedon**, to win the captains and soldiers that were there; and he also kept at his disposal all the young gentlemen of the Romans, whom he found in Athens studying philosophy: amongst them he found **Cicero's son**, whom he highly praised and commended, saying, that whether he waked or slept he found him of a noble mind and disposition, he did in nature so much hate tyrants.

Shortly after, he began to enter openly into arms: and being advertised that there came out of Asia a certain fleet of Roman ships that had good store of money in them, and that **the captain of those ships** (who was an honest man, and his familiar friend) came towards Athens, he went to meet him as far as **Carystus**, and having spoken with him there, he handled him so, that he was contented to leave his ships in Brutus' hands. Whereupon he made him a notable banquet at his house, because it was on his birthday. When the feast day came, and that they began to drink lustily one to another, the guests drank to the victory of Brutus, and the liberty of the Romans. Brutus therefore, to encourage them further, called for a bigger cup, and holding it in his hand, before he drank spoke this verse aloud:

"But fate my death and **Leto's son** have wrought."

And for proof hereof it is reported, that the same day he fought his last battle by the city of Philippi, as he came out of his tent he gave his men for the word and signal of battle, "Apollo": so that it was thought ever since that his sudden crying out at the feast was a **prognostication** of his misfortune that should happen.

Part Three

[omission for length: Brutus continued to collect military allies and money]

So when news was brought that **Gaius (Antony's brother)**, coming out of Italy, had passed the sea and came with great speed towards the city of **Dyrrhachium** and Apollonia, to get the soldiers into his hands which **Gabinius** had there: Brutus resolved to anticipate him, and to seize them first, and in all haste moved forwards with those he had about him. His march was very difficult, through rugged places and in a great show, but so swift that he left those that were to bring his provisions for the morning meal a great way behind.

[Brutus became ill near Dyrrhachium.]

Brutus growing very faint with his illness, and there being none in the whole army that had anything for him to eat, his servants were forced to have recourse to the enemy, and, going as far as to the gates of the city, begged bread of the sentinels that were upon duty. As soon as they heard of the condition of Brutus, they came themselves, and brought both meat and drink along with them; in return for which Brutus, when he took the city, showed the greatest kindness, not to them only, but to all the inhabitants, for their sakes.

[omission for length]

Narration and Discussion

How did Brutus show strength of character at this time?

Why did Brutus make such an odd toast during his party?

Creative Narration: Imagine that Brutus, instead of writing to Cicero, had the conversation with him in person. Write or act out the scene. **OR** Write a speech for Porcia on viewing the picture from *The Iliad*.

Lesson Five

Introduction

Mark Antony refused to lift the siege against Decimus Brutus (the cousin of Marcus Brutus) unless he received a number of demands (such as the government of Transalpine Gaul). Throughout the spring months of 43 B.C., Roman troops continued to move toward Mutina, hoping to end the siege or at least keep Decimus from surrendering to Antony. It was also reported that Dolabella had killed Trebonius in Smyrna, meaning that Dolabella was now declared a public enemy, and therefore Rome planned to send troops against him as well.

Octavius and the two consuls defeated Antony, but both consuls were killed, leaving Rome short of generals. In an unexpected turn of Senate decision-making, Marcus Brutus and Cassius were both given the governorships that had been promised but cancelled, and Cassius took over the campaign against Dolabella. Decimus, now that the siege was lifted, was put in charge of capturing Antony, with Octavius under his command (which did not please Octavius).

In the summer of 43 B.C., Decimus attempted to join Brutus in Macedon, but was killed (by Antony's orders) on his way there. Octavius, a bit afraid of Antony's power, but also nervous about the fickle support of the Senate, tried a new tactic: he returned to Rome and demanded the vacant consul seats for himself and one of his relatives. As consul, he cancelled the "public enemy" orders for both Antony and Marcus Aemilius Lepidus; and this allowed the three of them (that autumn) to legally form an alliance called the Second Triumvirate. Though not truly friends, they recognized their mutual desire for power, and the need for co-operation.

One of the first acts of the Triumvirate was to issue **proscriptions** (death sentences and seizures of property) against any and all political enemies. At the top of Antony's list was Cicero. Brutus and Cassius were also included, because of their involvement in the death of Julius Caesar; but as they were not close at hand (as Cicero was), they would have to be defeated and captured first.

Early in 42 B.C., Brutus and Cassius were reunited at Smyrna, and the last part of the reading describes their meeting.

Shakespeare Connections

"After that, these three, Octavius Caesar, Antony, and Lepidus **made an agreement between themselves**..." This occurs at the beginning of Act 4, Scene 1, where Antony also mentions that "Brutus and Cassius / Are levying powers." Brutus and Cassius discuss the proscriptions and the death of Cicero in Act 4, Scene 3. They also talk about the news Brutus has just received of Porcia's suicide ("she fell distract, / And (her attendants absent) swallow'd fire"). Plutarch does not mention this until the end of Brutus' *Life*, and he says there that her death may not have occurred in that manner or at that exact time. But it does seem probable that she died before Brutus, possibly by suicide, but perhaps of illness or grief.

Vocabulary

the noblest person in Rome: Julius Caesar

made an agreement…: formed the Second Triumvirate

lenity: mildness, gentleness

sundry, diverse: various

People

Gaius Antonius: see previous lesson

Pomponius Atticus: a close friend of Cicero

Historic Occasions

February 43 B.C.: A state of emergency was declared in Rome.

March-April 43 B.C.: Death of both consuls in battle against Antony

Summer 43 B.C.: Death of Decimus Brutus

August 43 B.C.: Octavius declared consul

October 43 B.C.: Formation of the Second Triumvirate

December 43 B.C.: Death of Cicero

January 42 B.C.: Julius Caesar posthumously declared divine by the Senate, allowing Octavius to declare himself "Son of the Divine"

January 42 B.C.: Roman troops sent against Brutus and Cassius

Early 42 B.C.: Brutus and Cassius met at **Smyrna**

On the Map

Bithynia: a Roman province in Anatolia, part of present-day Turkey

Cyzicus: a town in Anatolia

Syria: a Roman province which included the kingdom of Judea

Smyrna: An important city of Roman Asia, located on the Aegean Sea. Find **Smyrna** and **Sardis** (see the next lesson) on a historical map. (Try looking for a Bible map showing the Seven Churches of Asia.)

Reading

Part One

As Brutus prepared to go into Asia, news came unto him of the great change at Rome. For Octavius Caesar was in arms, by commandment and authority from the Senate, against Mark Antony. But after Octavius had driven Antony out of Italy, the Senate then began to be afraid of him Octavius: because he sued to be consul, which was contrary to the law, and kept a great army about him, when the empire of Rome had no need of them. On the other side, Octavius Caesar perceiving the Senate turned unto Brutus that was out of Italy, and that they appointed him the government of certain provinces: then he begun to be afraid for his part, and sent unto Antony to offer him his friendship. Then coming on with his army near to Rome, he made himself to be chosen consul, whether the Senate would or not, when he was yet but a young man of twenty years old, as he himself reporteth in his own *Commentaries*.

So, when he was consul, he presently appointed judges to accuse Brutus and his companions for killing of **the noblest person in Rome**, and chiefest Magistrate, without law or judgement: and made L. Cornificius accuse Brutus, and M. Agrippa, Cassius. So the parties accused were condemned, because the judges were compelled to give such sentence. The voice went, that when the herald (according to the custom after sentence given) went up to the chair or pulpit for orations, and proclaimed Brutus with a loud voice, summoning him to appear in person before the judges, the people that stood by sighed openly, and the noblemen that were present hung down their heads, and durst not speak a word. Among them, the tears fell from Publius Silicius' eyes: who, shortly after, was one of the proscripts or outlaws appointed to be slain.

After that, these three, Octavius Caesar, Antony, and Lepidus **made an agreement between themselves**, and by those articles, divided the provinces belonging to the Empire of Rome among themselves; and did set up bills of proscription and outlawry, condemning two hundred of the noblest men of Rome to suffer death; and among that number, Cicero was one.

[omission for length]

Part Two

Now when Brutus had passed over his army (that was very great) into Asia, he gave order for the gathering of a great number of ships together, as well in the coast of **Bithynia**, as also in the city of **Cyzicus**, because he would have an army by sea: and himself in the meantime went unto the cities, taking order for all things, and giving audience unto princes and noblemen of the country that had to do with him. Afterwards he sent unto Cassius in **Syria**, to turn him from his journey into Egypt, telling him that it was not for the conquest of any kingdom for themselves that they wandered up and down in that sort, but contrarily, that it was to restore their country again to their liberty: and that the multitude of soldiers they gathered together was to subdue the tyrants that would keep them in slavery and subjection. Wherefore, regarding their chief purpose and intent, they should not be far from Italy, as near as they could possible, but should rather make all the haste they could to help their countrymen. Cassius believed him, and returned.

Brutus went to meet him, and they both met at the city of **Smyrna**, which was the first time that they saw together since they took leave each of other in Athens: the one going into Syria, and the other into Macedon. So they were marvellous joyful, and no less courageous, when they saw the great armies together which they had both levied: considering that they departing out of Italy like naked and poor banished men, without armour and money, nor having any ship ready, nor soldier about them, nor any one town at their commandment: yet notwithstanding, in a short time after they were now met together, having ships, money, and soldiers enough, both footmen and horsemen, to fight for the empire of Rome.

Now Cassius would have done Brutus as much honour, as Brutus did unto him: but Brutus most commonly prevented him, and went first unto him, both because he was the elder man, as also for that he was sickly of body. And men reputed him commonly to be very skillful in wars, but otherwise marvellous choleric and cruel, who sought to rule men by fear, rather than with **lenity**: and on the other side he was too familiar with his friends, and would jest too broadly with them.

But Brutus in contrary manner, for his virtue and valiantness, was well-beloved of the people and his own, esteemed of noble men, and hated of no man, not so much as of his enemies: because he was a marvellous lowly and gentle person, noble-minded, and would never be in any rage, nor carried away with pleasure and covetousness, but had ever an upright mind with him, and would never yield to any wrong or injustice, the which was the chiefest cause of his fame, of his rising, and of the good will that every man bore him: for they were all persuaded that his intent was good.

For they did not certainly believe, that if Pompey himself had overcome Caesar he would have resigned his authority to the law: but rather they were of opinion that he would still keep the sovereignty and absolute government in his hands, taking only, to please the people, the title of consul or dictator, or of some other more civil office. And as for Cassius, a hot, choleric, and cruel man, that would oftentimes be carried away from justice for gain: it was certainly thought that he made war, and put himself into **sundry** dangers, more to have absolute power and authority, than to defend the liberty of his country. And in contrary manner, his enemies themselves did never reprove Brutus for any such change or desire. For it was said that Antony spoke it openly **divers** times, that he thought that of all them that had slain Caesar there was none but Brutus only, that was moved to do it as thinking the act commendable of itself; but that all the other conspirators did conspire his death, for some private malice or envy, that they otherwise did bear unto him. Hereby it appeareth that Brutus did not trust so much to the power of his army, as he did to his own virtue: as is to be seen by his writings. For approaching near to the instant danger, he wrote unto **Pomponius Atticus**, that his affairs had the best hap that could be. "For," said he, "either I will set my country at liberty by battle, or by honourable death rid me of this bondage." And furthermore, that they being certain and assured of all things else, this one thing only was doubtful to them: whether they should live or die with liberty. He wrote also that Antony had his due payment for his folly. For where he might have been a partner equally of the glory of Brutus, Cassius, and Cato, and have made one with them, he liked better to choose to be joined with Octavius Caesar alone: "With whom, though now he be not overcome by us, yet shall he shortly after also have war with him." And truly he proved Brutus a true prophet, for so came it indeed to pass.

Narration and Discussion

Describe the meeting of Brutus and Cassius at **Smyrna** (in a simple or more creative format). As you read **Lesson Six**, compare this with their next meeting at **Sardis**. Had things changed?

Lesson Six

Introduction

This lesson bridges two meetings between Brutus and Cassius: that at Smyrna, and that at Sardis. In between those points, the military crisis grew, and personal conflicts became more heated.

Shakespeare Connections

"About that time, Brutus sent to pray Cassius to come to the city of **Sardis**, and so he did. Brutus, understanding of his coming, went to meet him with all his friends." This occurs in Act 4, Scene 2.

"Then they began to pour out their complaints one to the other, and grew hot and loud..." "This Favonius at that time, in despite of the doorkeepers, came into the chamber..." This is dramatized in Act 4, Scene 3. (Note that Titinius is used here as one of the doorkeepers. He also appears briefly in the next scene.)

Vocabulary

rap and rend: snatch, seize

dissuaded him from it: tried to persuade him not to do it

behaved with no clemency: he treated the people there without mercy

engines of battery: battering rams

bade every man avoid: told everyone to stay out

Cynical: Cynicism was a form of Greek philosophy which had regained popularity in Rome at this time; but its followers (often outspoken) were often mocked as "pretend Cynics" (as Favonius is here).

People

Marcus Favonius: a Roman politician. Those who have read Plutarch's *Life of Pompey* may remember that he challenged Pompey to follow through on his promise to stomp his feet and produce an army. He was imprisoned and put to death after the **Battle of Philippi**.

Historic Occasions

June 42 B.C.: Brutus and Cassius met at **Sardis**

On the Map

city of the Xanthians or **Xanthos:** the oldest and largest city of the mountain province of **Lycia** (not to be confused with Lydia)

city of the Patareans: Patara, a city of Lycia, on the Mediterranean.

country of Ionia: a region of Anatolia

Sardis: an important city of the former Persian empire, and the capital of the kingdom of Lydia. It was considered a site of military strength.

Reading

Part One

Now, whilst Brutus and Cassius were together in the city of Smyrna, Brutus prayed Cassius to let him have some part of his money, whereof he had great store, because all that he could **rap and rend** of his side, he had bestowed it in making so great a number of ships, that by means of them they should keep all the sea at their commandment. Cassius' friends hindered this request, and earnestly **dissuaded him from it**: persuading him, that it was no reason that Brutus should have the money which Cassius had gotten together by sparing, and levied with great evil will of the people their subjects, for him to bestow liberally upon his soldiers, and by this means to win their goodwills by Cassius' charge. This notwithstanding, Cassius gave him the third part of his total sum.

So Cassius and Brutus then departing from each other, Cassius took the city of Rhodes, where he **behaved with no clemency**; although when he came into the city, he answered some of the inhabitants, who called him lord and king, that he was neither lord nor king, but he only that had slain him that would have been lord and king.

Brutus, departing from thence, sent unto the **Lycians** to require money, and men of war. But there was a certain orator, called Naucrates, that made the cities to rebel against him, insomuch that the countrymen of that country kept the straits and little mountains, thinking by that means to stop Brutus' passage. Wherefore Brutus sent his horsemen against them, who stole upon them as they were at dinner, and slew six hundred of them: and taking all the small towns and villages, he did let all the prisoners he took go without payment of ransom, hoping, by this his great courtesy to win them, to draw all the rest of the country unto him. But they were so fierce and obstinate, that they would mutiny for every small hurt they received as they passed by their country, and did despise his courtesy and good nature: until that at length he went to besiege the **city of the Xanthians**, within the which were shut up the cruelest and most warlike men of Lycia. There was a river that ran by the walls of the city, in the which many men saved themselves, swimming between two waters, and fled: howbeit they laid nets across the river, and tied little bells on the top of them, to sound when any man was taken in the nets. The Xanthians made a sally out by night, and came to fire certain **engines of battery** that beat down their walls: but they were presently driven in again by the Romans, so soon as they were discovered. The wind by chance was marvellous big, and increased the flame so sore, that it violently carried it into the crannies of the wall of the city, so that the next houses unto them were straight set afire thereby. Wherefore Brutus being afraid that all the city would be set on fire, he presently commanded his men to quench the fire, and to save the town if it might be.

But the Lycians at that instant fell into such a frenzy and strange and horrible despair, that no man can well express it: and a man cannot more rightly compare or liken it, than to a frantic and most desperate desire to die. For all of them together, with their wives and children, masters and servants, and of all sorts of age whatsoever, fought upon the rampart of their walls, and did cast down stones and fireworks on the Romans, which were very busy in quenching the flame of the fire to save the city. And in contrary manner also, they brought dry wood and reeds, to bring the fire further into the city as much as might be, increasing it by such things as they brought.

Now when the fire had gotten into all the parts of the city, and that the flame burnt bright in every place: Brutus, being sorry to see it, got upon his horse, and rode round about the walls of the city, to see if it were possible to save it, and held up his hands to the inhabitants, praying them to pardon their city, and to save themselves. Howbeit they would not be persuaded, but most of them killed themselves and their families.

[omission for content]

Therefore Brutus likewise besieging the **city of the Patareans**, and after they had thus yielded themselves, divers other cities also followed them, and did the like: and found Brutus more merciful and courteous than they thought they should have done, but specially far above Cassius. For Cassius, about the selfsame time, after he had compelled the Rhodians every man to deliver all the ready money they had in gold and silver in their houses, the which being brought together amounted to the sum of eight thousand talents: yet he condemned the city besides to pay the sum of five hundred talents more. Where Brutus in contrary manner, after he had levied of all the country of Lycia but a hundred and fifty talents only, he departed thence into the **country of Ionia**, and did them no more hurt.

[omission for length]

Part Two

About that time, Brutus sent to pray Cassius to come to the city of **Sardis**, and so he did. Brutus, understanding of his coming, went to meet him with all his friends. There, both their armies being armed, the soldiers called them both Emperors.

Now, as it commonly happeneth in great affairs between two persons, both of them having many friends and so many captains under them, there ran tales and complaints betwixt them. Therefore, before they fell in hand with any other matter, they went into a little chamber together, and **bade every man avoid**, and did shut the doors to them. Then they began to pour out their complaints one to the other, and grew hot and loud, earnestly accusing one another, and at length fell both the other, a-weeping. Their friends that were without the chamber hearing them loud within, and angry between themselves, they were both amazed, and afraid also lest it grow to further matter: but yet they were commanded, that no man should come to them. Notwithstanding, one **Marcus Favonius**, that had been a friend and follower of Cato while he lived, and, not so much by his learning or wisdom as by his wild, vehement manner, maintained the character of a philosopher, was rushing in upon them, but was hindered by the attendants. But it was a hard matter to stop Favonius, wherever his wildness hurried him; for he was fierce in all his behaviour, and ready to do anything to get his will. And though he was a senator, yet, thinking that one of the least of his excellences, he valued himself more upon a sort of **Cynical** liberty of speaking what he pleased, yet this boldness did no hurt many times, because they did but laugh at him to see him so mad. This Favonius at that time, in despite of the doorkeepers, came into the chamber, and with a certain scoffing and mocking gesture which he counterfeited of purpose, he rehearsed the verses which old Nestor said in Homer:

"Be ruled, for I am older than ye both."

Cassius fell a-laughing at him: but Brutus thrust him out of the chamber, and called him "dog," and "counterfeit Cynic." Howbeit his coming in broke their strife at that time, and so they left each other. The selfsame night Cassius prepared his supper in his chamber, and Brutus brought his friends with him. So, when they were set at supper, Favonius came to sit down after he had washed. Brutus told him aloud, no man sent for him, and bade them set him at the upper end, meaning indeed at the lower end of the couch. Favonius made no ceremony, but thrust in amongst the midst of them, and made all the company laugh at him: so they were merry all suppertime, and full of their philosophy.

Narration and Discussion

Explain the argument between Brutus and Cassius when they met at Sardis.

Why do you think that Brutus and Cassius allowed Favonius to come in and tease them, and sit where he wanted to at dinner?

For older students: Brutus is described as a merciful and courteous ruler. How is it then that the Xanthians refused to surrender to him? (You may want to look up something about the history of the Xanthians; apparently this was not the first time they had used an extreme strategy to protect themselves.)

Lesson Seven

Introduction

In matters of honesty, Brutus could be unyielding (perhaps like the previously-mentioned tempered steel). In other matters, however, he showed great insight into human behaviour and motivation: for example, understanding that providing excellent armour would help his soldiers "fight like devils." (In **Lesson Eight**, we read that he gave them a financial incentive as well.) In this passage, we read that Brutus also struggled with "demons" of fear and uncertainty, which manifested themselves as a ghostly visitor in his tent.

Shakespeare Connections

"… Brutus publicly disgraced and condemned Lucius Pella…This judgement was much misliked by Cassius: for but a few days before, two of his own friends being accused of the same crime, he only admonished them in private, but in public absolved them…." Cassius complains about this in Act 4, Scene 3.

"Brutus, in contrary manner, answered that he should remember the Ides of March." In Shakespeare's scene, Brutus says, "Remember March, the ides of March remember."

"So Brutus boldly asked what he was, a god or a man, and what cause brought him thither. The spirit answered him, 'I am thy evil spirit, Brutus: and thou shalt see me by the city of **Philippi**." This also takes place in Act 4, Scene 3.

"But just as the troops were going on board, there came two eagles…" Cassius mentions this in Act 5, Scene 1.

Vocabulary

embezzled: stolen

absolved: forgave

by his countenance: by his allowing of those things to happen

despatching of his weightiest causes: dealing with important business

Epicurean: The Epicurean philosophy stated that the highest good was pleasure; but it also promoted freedom from fear.

driven to forsake…: Norbanus retreated towards **Amphipolis.**

rich furniture: equipment; the things the army was "furnished" with

People

Norbanus: Gaius Norbanus Flaccus, a Roman politician and general

Historic Occasions

Autumn 42 B.C.: Preparations for battle

On the Map

Philippi: a Greek city which had been conquered first by the Macedonians (and renamed for Philip II), and then by the Romans. The **Philippian Fields** were the plain to the west of the city.

Thasos: or Thassos; a large Greek island

Amphipolis: a city in the Roman province of Thrace, considered a stronghold for occupying armies.

Reading

Part One

The next day after, upon the accusation of the Sardians, Brutus publicly disgraced and condemned Lucius Pella, one that had been employed in offices of trust by himself, for having **embezzled** the public money. This judgement was much misliked by Cassius: for but a few days before, two of his own friends being accused of the same crime, he only admonished them in private, but in public **absolved** them, and continued them in his service. And therefore he greatly reproved Brutus, for that he would show himself so strait and severe, in such a time as was meeter to bear a little, than to take things at the worst. Brutus, in contrary manner, answered that

> he should remember the Ides of March, at which
> time they slew Julius Caesar: who neither
> plundered nor pillaged the country, but only was
> the support and strength of all them that did rob
> and spoil **by his countenance** and authority. And

if there were any occasion whereby they might honestly set aside justice and equity, they should have had more reason to have suffered Caesar's friends to have robbed and done what wrong and injury they had would, than to bear with their own men. "For then," said he, "they could but have said they had been cowards: and now they may accuse us of injustice, beside the pains we take, and the danger we put ourselves into."

And thus may we see what Brutus' intent and purpose was.

Part Two

But as they both prepared to pass over again out of Asia into Europe, there went a rumour that there appeared a wonderful sign unto him. Brutus was a careful man, and slept very little, both for that his diet was moderate, as also because he was continually occupied. He never slept in the daytime, and in the night no longer than the time he was driven to be alone, and when everybody else took their rest. But now whilst he was in war, and his head ever busily occupied to think of his affairs, and care and what would happen: after he had slumbered a little after supper, he spent all the rest of the night in **despatching of his weightiest causes**; and after he had taken order for them, if he had any leisure left him, he would read some book till the third watch of the night, at what time the centurions and tribunes did use to come unto him for orders. So, one night very late (when all the camp took quiet rest) as he was in his tent with a little light, thinking of weighty matters: he thought he heard one come in to him, and casting his eye towards the door of his tent, that he saw a wonderful strange and monstrous shape of a body coming towards him, and said never a word. So Brutus boldly asked what he was, a god or a man, and what cause brought him thither. The spirit answered him, "I am thy evil spirit, Brutus: and thou shalt see me by the city of **Philippi**." Brutus, being no otherwise afraid, replied again unto it: "Well, then I shall see thee again."

The spirit presently vanished away, and Brutus called his men unto him, who told him that they heard no noise, nor saw anything at all. Thereupon Brutus returned again to think on his matters as he did before: and when the day broke, he went unto Cassius, to tell him what vision had appeared unto him in the night. Cassius being in opinion an **Epicurean**, and reasoning thereon with Brutus, spoke to him touching the vision thus:

> "In our sect, Brutus, we have an opinion, that we do not always feel or see that which we suppose we do both see and feel...For our imagination doth upon a small fancy grow from conceit to conceit, altering both in passions and forms of things imagined. For the mind of man is ever occupied, and that continual moving is nothing but an imagination. But yet there is a further cause of this in you. For you being by nature given to melancholic discoursing, and of late continually occupied, your wits and senses, having been over-laboured, do more easily yield to such imaginations. For, to say that there are spirits or angels, and if there were, that they had the shape of men, or such voices, or any power at all to come unto us: it is a mockery. And for mine own part I would there were such, because that we should not only have soldiers, horses, and ships, but also the aid of the gods, to guide and further our honest and honourable attempts."

With these words Cassius did somewhat comfort and quiet Brutus. But just as the troops were going on board, there came two eagles that, flying with a marvellous force, lighted upon two of the foremost ensigns; and always followed the soldiers, which gave them meat and fed them, until they came near to the city of Philippi; and there, one day only before the battle, they both flew away.

Part Three

Now Brutus had conquered the most part of all the people and nations of that country: but if there were any other city or captain to overcome, then they made all clear before them; and so drew towards the coasts of **Thasos**. There **Norbanus** lying in camp in a certain place called the Straits, Cassius and Brutus compassed him in in such sort, that he was

driven to forsake the place which was of great strength for him, and he was also in danger beside to have lost all his army. For Octavius Caesar could not follow him because of his sickness, and therefore stayed behind: whereupon they would have taken his army, if not for Antony's aid, which made such wonderful speed that Brutus could scant believe it. Caesar came up ten days after; and Antony camped against Cassius, and Brutus on the other side against Caesar.

The Romans called the valley between both camps the **Philippian Fields:** and there were never seen two so great armies of the Romans, one before the other, ready to fight. In truth, Brutus' army was inferior to Octavius Caesar's, in number of men: but for bravery and **rich furniture**, Brutus' army far excelled Caesar's. For the most part of their armours were silver and gilt, which Brutus had bountifully given them: although in all other things he taught his captains to live in order without excess. But for the bravery of armour which soldiers should carry in their hands, or otherwise wear upon their backs: he thought that it was an encouragement unto them that by nature are greedy of honour, and that it maketh them also fight like devils, that love to get, and be afraid to lose: because they fight to keep their armour and weapon, as also their goods and lands.

Narration and Discussion

When the spirit warned Brutus that he would see him by the city of Philippi, Brutus replied with the equivalent of "Okay, see you then." Was he just being flippant? Why did he not appear more concerned?

Creative Narration: As a reporter, describe the ways that Brutus and Cassius were preparing to fight the **Battle of Philippi**. At this point, would you predict success or defeat for them?

Lesson Eight

Introduction

Certain omens began to appear, worrying Cassius to the point that he suggested delaying the fighting as long as possible. Brutus, on the other hand, wanted to have the whole thing over with as quickly as possible.

Shakespeare Connections

In an omitted section, Plutarch describes "the superstitious fears which were gradually carrying even Cassius himself away from his Epicurean doctrines…" In Act 5, Scene I, Cassius says, "You know that I held Epicurus strong, / And his opinion; now I change my mind,/ And partly credit things that do presage." However, he is determined to see it through. Plutarch's Cassius says to Messalla, "And yet we must be lively, and of good courage, considering our good fortune, whom we should wrong too much to mistrust her, although we follow evil counsel." In Shakespeare's version, Cassius says, "For I am fresh of spirit, and resolv'd / To meet all perils very constantly."

Plutarch's Cassius says, "For either we shall conquer, or we shall not need to fear the conquerors"; but Shakespeare gives Brutus similar words to end the scene: "But it sufficeth that the day will end, / And then the end is known." You may want to discuss why Shakespeare's instinct for good theatre would lead him to make that change.

Vocabulary

muster: assemble in preparation for battle

purify it in the fields: perform a rite of cleansing from past wrongs

drachma: silver coin

wether: male sheep

skirmishes and bickerings: minor battles

jeopardy: risk

mistrust her: Fortune, to the Romans, was a female deity

Providence: God, or, the gods

fell a-laughing: Dryden says "smiled"

People

Messalla (sometimes spelled Messala): Marcus Valerius Messalla Corvinus, a Roman general and writer. Also referred to as Corvinus.

Reading

Part One

Now, when they came to **muster** their armies, Octavius Caesar took the muster of his army within the trenches of his camp, and gave his men only a little corn, and five silver drachmas to every man to sacrifice to the gods, and to pray for victory. But Brutus scorning this poverty and meanness of spirit, first of all mustered his army, and did **purify it in the fields**, according to the manner of the Romans: and then he gave unto every band a number of **wethers** to sacrifice, and fifty silver drachmas to every soldier. So that Brutus' and Cassius' soldiers were better pleased, and more courageously bent to fight at the day of the battle, than their enemies' soldiers were.

[omission for length]

But, perceiving that in the daily **skirmishes and bickerings** they made, his men were always the stronger, and ever had the better: that yet quickened his spirits again, and did put him in better heart. And furthermore, because that some of their own men had already yielded themselves to their enemies, and that it was suspected moreover divers others would do the like: that made many of Cassius' friends, which were of his mind before, (when it came to be debated in council whether the battle should be fought or not), that they were then of Brutus' mind. But yet was there one of Brutus' friends called Atellius, that was against it, and was of opinion that they should tarry the next winter. Brutus asked him what he should get by tarrying a year longer? "If I get nought else," quoth Atellius again, "yet have I lived so much longer." Cassius was very angry with this answer: and Atellius was maliced and esteemed the worse for it of all men. Thereupon it was presently determined they should fight battle the next day.

So Brutus all suppertime looked with a cheerful countenance, like a man that had good hope, and talked very wisely of philosophy, and after supper went to bed.

But touching Cassius, **Messalla** reporteth that he supped by himself in his tent with a few of his friends, and that all suppertime he looked very sadly, and was full of thoughts, although it was against his nature: and that after supper he took him by the hand, and holding him fast (in token of kindness as his manner was) told him in Greek: "Messalla, I protest unto thee, and make thee my witness, that I am compelled against my mind and will (as Pompey the great was) to **jeopardy** the liberty of our country to the hazard of a battle. And yet we must be lively, and of good courage, considering our good fortune, whom we should wrong too much to **mistrust her**, although we follow evil counsel." Messalla writeth, that Cassius having spoken these last words unto him, he bade him farewell, and willed him to come to supper to him the next night following, because it was his birthday.

Part Two

The next morning, by break of day, the signal of battle was set out in Brutus' and Cassius' camp, which was a scarlet coat: and both the chieftains spoke together in the midst of their armies. There Cassius began to speak first, and said:

> "The gods grant us, O Brutus, that this day we may
> win the field, and ever after to live all the rest of our
> life quietly, one with another. But since the gods
> have so ordained it, that the greatest and chiefest
> things amongst men are most uncertain, and that if
> the battle fall out otherwise to-day than we wish or
> look for, we shall hardly meet again: what art thou
> then determined to do, to fly, or die?"

Brutus answered him,

> "Being yet but a young man, and not over greatly
> experienced in the world, I trust (I know not how) a
> certain rule of philosophy, by the which I did greatly
> blame and reprove Cato for killing of himself, as
> being no lawful nor godly act, touching the gods,
> nor, concerning men valiant; not to evade the divine

48

course of things, and not fearlessly to receive and undergo the evil that shall happen, but run away from it. But now in my own fortunes I am of another mind; for if **Providence** shall not dispose what we now undertake according to our wishes, I will look no more for hope, neither seek to make any new supply for war again, but will rid me of this miserable world, and content me with my fortune. For I gave up my life for my country in the Ides of March, for the which I shall live in another more glorious world."

Cassius **fell a-laughing** to hear what he said, and embracing him, "Come on then," said he, "let us go and charge our enemies with this mind. For either we shall conquer, or we shall not need to fear the conquerors."

Narration and Discussion

Compare Plutarch's account of the discussion between Brutus and Cassius to Shakespeare's adaptation (Julius Caesar, Act 5, Scene 1) (see below). Is Shakespeare faithful to the spirit of the conversation as Plutarch tells it? How do you feel about the changes he has made?

For older students: Brutus planned to kill himself if this battle were lost. What hope does the Bible offer those who face deep despair?

Creative Narration: Continue the reporting begun in **Lesson Seven**.

Lesson Nine

Introduction

The battle began, and Brutus and Cassius led their soldiers in different directions. Brutus' troops managed to plunder Caesar's camp; however, miscommunication and careless mistakes led to tragedy.

Shakespeare Connections

In Act 5, Scene 3, Shakespeare uses the dramatic device of having Cassius and others narrate what they see, rather than trying to replicate an entire battle onstage.

Plutarch mentions the character Titinius only in this passage: "Cassius sent Titinius, one of them that was with him, to go and know what they were. Brutus' horsemen saw him coming afar off…they shouted out for joy…and went and embraced him…Cassius thought that Titinius was actually taken by the enemy…and slew himself." In the play, Titinius returns and finds Cassius' body, then takes his own life. You may want to discuss how and why Shakespeare expanded on Plutarch's "minor" characters.

At the end of Act 5, Scene 3, Brutus says, "Ere night / We shall try fortune in a second fight," referring to the second battle (although it did not actually take place on the same day).

Vocabulary

> **cast a trench:** dig a ditch
>
> **little bills:** handbills; notes. Those who have read *Alice in Wonderland* may recall the title of Chapter IV, "The Rabbit Sends in a Little Bill."
>
> **word of the battle:** the signal (see the **Top Ten Vocabulary Terms**)
>
> **the voward:** those at the front
>
> **other ensigns:** To steal the standard (or "capture the flag") of the enemy was considered a sign of victory.
>
> **brake immediately:** broke their ranks and fled

People

> **Lacedaemonians:** Spartans

Historic Occasions

October 3, 42 B.C.: First battle at Philippi; death of Cassius

Reading

Part One

After this talk, they fell to consultation among their friends for the ordering of the battle. Then Brutus prayed Cassius he might have the leading of the right wing, the which men thought was far meeter for Cassius: both because he was the elder man, and also for that he had the better experience. But yet Cassius gave it him, and willed that Messalla (who had charge of one of the warlikest legions they had) should be also in that wing with Brutus. So Brutus presently sent out his horsemen, who were excellently well appointed, and his footmen also were as willing and ready to give charge.

Now Antony' men did **cast a trench** from the marsh by the which they lay, to cut off Cassius' way to come to the sea. Caesar was to be at hand with his troops to support them, but he was not able to be present himself, by reason of his sickness. And for his soldiers, they little thought the enemies would have given them battle, but only have made some light skirmishes to hinder them that wrought in the trench, and with their darts and slings, to have kept them from finishing of their work; but they, taking no heed to them that came full upon them to give them battle, marvelled much at the great noise they heard, that came from the place where they were casting their trench.

In the meantime Brutus, that led the right wing, sent **little bills** to the colonels and captains of private bands, on which he wrote the **word of the battle**; and he himself, riding a-horseback by all the troops, did speak to them, and encouraged them to stick to it like men; but very few of them understood what was the word of the battle; and, besides, the most part of them never tarried to have it told them, but ran with great fury to assail the enemies: whereby, through this disorder, the legions were marvellously scattered and dispersed one from the other.

For first of all, Messalla's legion, and then the next unto them, went beyond the left wing of the enemies, and did nothing, but glancing by them overthrew some as they went, and so going on further fell right upon Caesar's camp *although he was not there himself, having been warned by a friend's dream.* There was great slaughter in this camp. For amongst others there were slain two thousand **Lacedaemonians**, who were arrived but even a little before, coming to aid Caesar.

The rest of the army, that had not gone round, but had engaged the front, easily overthrew them, finding them in great disorder; and slew upon the place three legions; and being carried on with the stream of victory, pursuing those that fled, fell into the camp with them, Brutus himself being there. But that which the conquerors thought not of, occasion shewed it unto them that were overcome: and that was, the left wing of their enemies left naked, and unguarded of them of the right wing, who were strayed too far off, in following of them that were overthrown. So they gave a hot charge upon them. But notwithstanding all the force they made, they could not break into the midst of their battle, where they found men that received them and valiantly made head against them. Howbeit they brake and overthrew the left wing where Cassius was, by reason of the great disorder among them, and also because they had no intelligence how the right wing had sped. So they chased them, beating them into their camp, the which they spoiled, none of both the chieftains being present there.

For Antony, as it is reported, to fly the fury of the first charge, was gotten into the next marsh: and no man could tell what became of Octavius Caesar, after he was carried out of his camp. Insomuch that there were certain soldiers that shewed their swords bloodied, and said that they had slain him, and did describe his face, and shewed what age he was of. Furthermore, **the voward** and the midst of Brutus' battle had already put all their enemies to flight that withstood them, with great slaughter: so that Brutus had conquered all of his side, and Cassius had lost all on the other side.

For nothing undid them, but that Brutus went not to help Cassius, thinking he had overcome them, as himself had done: and Cassius on the other side tarried not for Brutus, thinking he had been overthrown, as himself was. And to prove that the victory fell on Brutus' side, Messalla confirmeth it, that they won three eagles, and divers **other ensigns** of their enemies, and their enemies won never a one of theirs.

Part Two

Now Brutus returning from the chase, after he had slain and sacked Caesar's men, he wondered much that he could not see Cassius' tent standing up high as it was wont, neither the other tents of his camp standing as they were before, because all the whole camp had been spoiled, and the tents thrown down, at the first coming in of the enemies. But they that were about Brutus, whose sight served them better, told him that they saw a great glistering of harness, and a number of silvered targets, that went and came into Cassius' camp, and were not (as they took it) the armours nor the number of men that they had left there to guard the camp: and yet that they saw not such a number of dead bodies, and great overthrow, as there should have been if so many legions had been slain. This made Brutus at the first mistrust that which had happened. So he appointed a number of men to keep the camp of his enemy which he had taken, and caused his men to be sent for that yet followed the chase, and gathered them together, thinking to lead them to aid Cassius, who was in this state as you shall hear.

First of all he was marvellous angry to see how Brutus' men ran to give charge upon their enemies, and tarried not for the word of the battle nor commandment to give charge; and it grieved him beside, that after he had overcome them, his men fell straight to spoil, and were not careful to surround the rest of the enemies behind. But with tarrying too long also, more than through the valiantness or foresight of the captains his enemies, Cassius found himself surrounded by the right wing of his enemies' army. Whereupon his horsemen **brake immediately**, and fled for life towards the sea.

Furthermore, perceiving his footmen to give ground, he did what he could to keep them from fleeing, and took an ensign from one of the ensign-bearers that fled, and stuck it fast at his feet: although with much ado he could scant keep his own guard together. So Cassius himself was at length compelled to fly with a few about him, unto a little hill, from whence they might easily see what was done in all the plain: howbeit Cassius himself saw nothing, for his sight was very bad, saving that he saw (and yet with much ado) how the enemies spoiled his camp before his eyes.

He saw also a great troop of horsemen, whom Brutus sent to aid him, and thought that they were his enemies that followed him: but yet he sent Titinius, one of them that was with him, to go and know what they were. Brutus' horsemen saw him coming afar off, whom when they knew that he was one of Cassius' chiefest friends, they shouted out for joy: and they that were familiarly acquainted with him, lighted from their horses, and went and embraced him. The rest compassed him in round about a-horseback, with songs of victory and great rushing of their harness, so that they made all the field ring again for joy.

But this marred all. For Cassius thinking indeed that Titinius was taken of the enemies, he then spoke these words: "Desiring too much to live, I have lived to see one of my best friends taken, for my sake, before my face." After that, he got into a tent where nobody was, and commanded his servant Pindarus to kill him.

After that time Pindarus was never seen more. Whereupon some took occasion to say, that he had slain his master without his commandment. By and by they knew the horsemen that came towards them, and might see Titinius crowned with a garland of triumph, who came before with great speed unto Cassius. But when he perceived by the cries and tears of his friends which tormented themselves, the misfortunate that had chanced to his captain Cassius, by mistaking: he Titinius drew out his sword, cursing himself a thousand times that he had tarried so long, and so slew himself presently in the field.

Narration and Discussion

What were some of the reasons for the misunderstanding and chaos during this battle? Who actually won?

Our "limited vision" sometimes causes us to misunderstand people or events that God sends to help us. How might this story remind you to look for God's perspective in the events of your life?

Creative Narration: Continue the activity begun in **Lesson Seven.**

Lesson Ten

Introduction

As the only commanding officer, Brutus had to deal with a) a camp full of enemy prisoners, b) Cassius' defeated and discouraged soldiers, and c) the constant threat of desertion and rebellion from his own men. To make things worse, Antony and Octavius Caesar were making plans for a second battle, which they did not intend to lose.

Vocabulary

destitute: lacking

betimes: early

sack and spoil: treasure, loot

tempest: storm

tickle: uncertain

stubborn and lusty: hard to control

God: Dryden says "the divine power"

Historic Occasions

October 23, 42 B.C.: Second battle at Philippi; death of Brutus

Reading

Part One

Brutus in the meantime came forward still, and understood also that Cassius had been overthrown: but he knew nothing of his death till he came very near to his camp.

So when he was come thither, after he had lamented the death of Cassius, calling him the last of all the Romans, being impossible that

Rome should ever breed again so noble and valiant a man as he: he sent away the body to be buried at Thasos, lest celebrating his funeral within the camp might breed some disorder.

Then he called his soldiers together, and did encourage them again; and, seeing them **destitute** of all things necessary, he promised to every man two thousand drachmas in recompense of what he had lost. After his soldiers had heard his oration, they were all of them prettily cheered again, wondering much at his great liberality, and waited upon him with great cries when he went his way, praising him for that he only of the four chieftains was not overcome in battle. And to speak the truth, his deeds showed that he hoped not in vain to be conqueror. For with few legions he had slain and driven all them away, that made head against him: and yet if all his people had fought, and that the most of them had not outgone their enemies to run to spoil their goods, surely it was like enough he had slain them all, and had left never a man of them alive.

There were slain of Brutus' side about eight thousand men, counting the soldiers' slaves; and of the enemies' side, as Messalla writeth, there were slain, as he supposeth, more than twice as many more. Wherefore they were more discouraged than Brutus, until that very late at night there was one of Cassius' men called Demetrius who went unto Antony, and carried his master's clothes, whereof he was stripped not long before, and his sword also. This encouraged Brutus' enemies, and made them so brave, that the next morning **betimes** they stood in battle array again before Brutus. But, on Brutus' side, both his camps stood wavering, and that in great danger. For his own camp, being full of prisoners, required a good guard to look unto them: and Cassius' camp on the other side took the death of their captain very heavily, and besides, there was some vile grudge between them that were overcome and those that did overcome. For this cause therefore Brutus did set them in battle array, but yet kept himself from giving battle.

[omission for length]

Part Two

Afterwards Brutus performed the promise he had made to the soldiers, and gave them the two thousand drachmas apiece, but yet he first reproved them, because they went and gave charge upon the enemies at the first battle, before they had the word of battle given them: and made them a new promise also, that if in the second battle they fought like men, he would give them the **sack and spoil** of two cities, to wit, Thessalonica and Lacedaemon. In all Brutus' life there is but this only fault to be found, and that is not to be gainsaid (though Antony and Octavius Caesar did reward their soldiers far worse for their victory. For when they had driven all the natural Italians out of Italy, they gave their soldiers their lands and towns, to the which they had no right: and moreover, the only mark they shot at in all this war they made was but to overcome, and reign. Where in contrary manner they had so great an opinion of Brutus' virtue, that the common voice and opinion of the world would not suffer him neither to overcome, nor to save himself otherwise than justly and honestly, and specially after Cassius' death: whom men burdened, that oftentimes he moved Brutus to great cruelty.) But now, like as the mariners on the sea after the rudder of their ship is broken by **tempest**, do seek to nail on some other piece of wood in its place, and do help themselves to keep them from hurt as much as may be upon that instant danger: even so Brutus having such a great army to govern, and his affairs standing very **tickle**, and having no other captain coequal with him in dignity and authority: he was forced to employ them he had, and likewise to be ruled by them in many things, and was of mind himself also to grant them anything, that he thought might make them serve like noble soldiers at time of need. For Cassius' soldiers were very evil to be ruled, and did shew themselves very **stubborn and lusty** in the camp, because they had no chieftain that did command them: but yet rank cowards to their enemies, because they had once overcome them.

Part Three

On the other side Octavius Caesar and Antony were not in much better state: for first of all, they lacked victuals. And because they were lodged in low places, they looked to abide a hard and sharp winter, being camped as they were by the marsh side, and also for that after the battle there had fallen plenty of rain about the autumn, all their tents were full of mire and water, which through the coldness of the weather immediately froze. But beside all these discommodities, there came news unto them of the great loss they had of their men by sea. For Brutus' ships met with a great aid and supply of men, which were sent to Caesar's aid out of Italy, and they overthrew them in such sort, that there escaped but few of them: and yet they were so famished, that they were compelled to eat the tackle and sails of their ships. Thereupon Caesar and Antony were very desirous to fight a battle again *before* Brutus should have intelligence of this good news for him: for it chanced so, that the battle was fought by sea on the selfsame day it was fought by land. But by ill fortune, rather than through the malice or negligence of the captains, this victory came not to Brutus' ear till twenty days after. For had he known of it before, he would not have been brought to have fought a second battle, considering that he had excellent good provision for his army for a long time, and, besides, his army lay in a place of great strength, so as his camp could not be greatly hurt by the winter, nor also distressed by his enemies; and his being absolute master of the sea, and having at land overcome on that side wherein he himself was engaged, would have made him full of hope and confidence.

Howbeit the state of Rome (in my opinion) being now brought to that pass, that it could no more abide to be governed by many lords, but required one only absolute governor, **God**, to prevent Brutus that it should not come to his government, kept this victory from his knowledge, though indeed it came but a little too late.

For the day before the last battle was given, very late in the night, came Clodius, one of his enemies, into his camp, who told that Caesar, hearing of the overthrow of his army by sea, desired nothing more than to fight a battle before Brutus understood it. Howbeit they gave no credit to his words, but despised him so much that they would not vouchsafe to bring him unto Brutus, because they thought it was but a lie devised, to be the better welcome for this good news.

The selfsame night, it is reported that the monstrous spirit which had appeared before unto Brutus in the city of Sardis, did now appear again unto him in the selfsame shape and form, and so vanished away, and said never a word.

[omission for length and content]

Narration and Discussion:

Discuss this passage: "And to speak the truth, his deeds showed that he hoped not in vain to be conqueror. For with few legions he had slain and driven all them away, that made head against him: and yet if all his people had fought, and that the most of them had not outgone their enemies to run to spoil their goods, surely it was like enough he had slain them all, and had left never a man of them alive." Do you agree that Brutus' bravery is not lessened by the fact that he was hindered by deserters and men more interested in looting than in fighting? How might history have been changed if he had been backed up by soldiers as faithful as he was himself?

For older students: Plutarch says that "**God**, to prevent Brutus that it should not come to his government, kept this victory from his knowledge, though indeed it came but a little too late." Although we may not understand "God" or "divine power" in the same way as Plutarch did, his idea is an interesting one. Do you think God had a reason for wanting the Roman Empire to develop as it did at that time?

Lesson Eleven

Introduction

In this lesson we are shown two contrasting characters: **Camulatius**, a soldier who openly defected to the other side; and **Lucilius**, who showed the utmost loyalty to his commander.

Shakespeare Connections

The story of Lucilius is dramatized in Act 5, Scene 4.

Vocabulary

to tell him so much as he thought: to confirm his suspicion

faintly: without much enthusiasm

compass: surround

overharried: attacked repeatedly and on all sides

barbarous men: often foreigners, but here it may simply mean enemy
soldiers

happy: fortunate

booty: loot, prize

People

Camulatius: or Camulatus. We do not seem to have more information
about him, other than that he was a "good soldier."

the son of M. Cato: see **Lesson One**; Brutus' cousin and also the
brother of Brutus' wife Porcia

Reading

Part One

Now, after that Brutus had brought his army into the field, and had set
them second in battle ray, directly against the voward of his enemy: he
paused a long time, before he gave the signal of battle. For Brutus
riding up and down to view the bands and companies, it came in his
head to mistrust some of them, besides that some came **to tell him so
much as he thought**. Moreover, he saw his horsemen set forward but
faintly, and did not go lustily to give charge, but still stayed to see what
the footmen would do. Then suddenly, one of the chiefest knights he
had in all his army, called **Camulatius**, and that was always
marvellously esteemed of for his valiantness until that time: he came
hard by Brutus a-horseback, and rode, before his face, to yield himself
unto his enemies. Brutus was marvellous sorry for it: wherefore, partly
for anger, and partly for fear of greater treason and rebellion, he
suddenly caused his army to march, being past three of the clock in the
afternoon. So in that place where he himself fought in person, he had
the better, and broke into the left wing of his enemies, which gave him
way, through the help of his horsemen that gave charge with his

footmen, when they saw the enemies in amazement and afraid. Howbeit the other also on the right wing, when the Captains would have had them to have marched: they were afraid to have been **compassed** in behind, because they were fewer in number than their enemies, and therefore did spread themselves, and leave the midst of their battle. Whereby they having weakened themselves, they could not withstand the force of their enemies, but turned tail straight, and fled. And those that had put them to flight came straight upon it to compass Brutus behind, who in the midst of the conflict did all that was possible for a skillful captain and valiant soldier: both for his wisdom, as also for his hardiness, for the obtaining of victory.

But that which won him the victory at the first battle did now lose it him at the second. For at the first time, the enemies that were broken and fled were straight cut in pieces: but at the second battle, of Cassius' men that were put to flight, there were few slain: and they that saved themselves by speed, being afraid because they had been overcome, did discourage the rest of the army when they came to join with them, and filled all the army with fear and disorder. There was **the son of M. Cato** slain, valiantly fighting amongst the lusty youths. For, notwithstanding that he was very weary, and **overharried**, yet would he not therefore flee, but manfully fighting and laying about him, telling aloud his name, and also his father's name, at length he was beaten down amongst many other dead bodies of his enemies, which he had slain round about him. So there were slain in the field all the chiefest gentlemen and nobility that were in his army, who valiantly ran into any danger to save Brutus' life.

Part Two

*[The historian Appian says that the soldiers of Octavius now "seized the gate" of Brutus' camp, and that they formed patrols to capture anyone attempting to flee. Brutus himself, according to Appian, was pursued by enemy soldiers, and fled into the hills. This is the point at which **Lucilius** decided to act.]*

Amongst them there was one of Brutus' friends called **Lucilius**, who seeing a troop of **barbarous men** making no reckoning unto of all men else they met in their way, but going all together right against Brutus, he determined to stay them with the hazard of his life, and, being left behind, told them that *he* was Brutus: and, because they should believe him, he prayed them to bring him to Antony, for he said he was afraid of Caesar, and that he did trust Antony better. These barbarous men being very glad of this good hap, and thinking themselves **happy** men, they carried him in the night, and sent some before unto Antony, to tell him of their coming. He was marvellous glad of it, and went out to meet them that brought him. Others also understanding of it, that they had brought Brutus prisoner: they came out of all parts of the camp to see him, some pitying his hard fortune, and others saying, that it was not done like himself, so cowardly to be taken alive of the barbarous people for fear of death. When they came near together, Antony stayed awhile, bethinking himself how he should use Brutus.

In the meantime Lucilius was brought to him, who stoutly, with a bold countenance, said,

> "Antony, I dare assure thee that no enemy hath
> taken nor shall take Marcus Brutus alive: and I
> beseech God keep him from that fortune. For
> wheresoever he be found, alive or dead, he will
> found like himself. And now for myself, I am come
> unto thee, having deceived these men of arms here,
> bearing them down that I was Brutus: and do not
> refuse to suffer any torment thou wilt put me to."

Lucilius' words made them all amazed that heard him. Antony on the other side, looking upon all them that had brought him, said:

> "My companions, I think ye are sorry you have
> failed of your purpose, and that you think this man
> hath done you great wrong: but I do assure you, you
> have taken a better **booty** than that you followed.
> For, instead of an enemy, you have brought me a
> friend: and for my part, if you had brought me
> Brutus alive, truly I cannot tell what I should have
> done to him. For I had rather have such men my
> friends as this man here, than enemies."

Then he embraced Lucilius, and at that time delivered him to one of his friends in custody, and Lucilius ever after served him faithfully, even to his death.

Narration and Discussion

Why did Lucilius pretend to be Brutus? Look up John 15:13 (Greater love has no man than this...).

For older students: Those with a cynical turn of mind might ask if Lucilius was merely saving his own skin by finding a way into Antony's camp and appearing loyal and honourable (rather than, perhaps, accompanying Brutus on his escape). What do you think?

Creative Narration: This would be a good story to act out or to illustrate.

Lesson Twelve and Examination Questions

Introduction

Outmaneuvered by his enemies, there was not much that Brutus could do. "I do not complain of my fortune," he said, "but only for my country's sake: for, as for me, I think myself happier than they that have overcome."

Shakespeare Connections

Shakespeare dramatizes the final hour of Brutus' life in Act 5, Scene 5.

Vocabulary

firmament: the heavens

rehearsed: recited

Jove: Jupiter

posterity: those that come afterward

mantle: cloak

People

>Clitus, Dardanus, Flavius, Labeo, Statilius, Strato, Volumnius:
>Brutus' friends and fellow soldiers. Those who have read Plutarch's
>*Life of Cato the Younger* will remember the loyalty of Statilius to Cato in
>the last days of his life.

Historic Occasions

>October 23, 42 B.C.: death of Brutus

>31 B.C.: Battle of Actium, fought between the forces of Octavius
>Caesar and Mark Antony (plus Cleopatra). It is considered the end of
>the Roman Republic and the beginning of the Empire.

Reading

Part One

Now Brutus having passed a little river, walled in on either side with high rocks, and shadowed with great trees, being then dark night, he went no further, but stayed at the foot of a rock with certain of his captains and friends that followed him: and looking up to the firmament that was full of stars, sighing, he rehearsed two verses; one of which, Volumnius writes, was this:

>Punish, great Jove, the author of these ills.

The other, he says he has forgot.

Within a little while after, naming his friends that he had seen slain in battle before his eyes, he fetched a greater sigh than before: specially when he came to name Labeo and Flavius, of the which the one was his lieutenant, and the other chief officer of his engineers.

In the meantime, one of the company being athirst, and seeing Brutus athirst also: he ran to the river for water, and brought it in his helmet. At the selfsame time they heard a noise on the other side of the river. Whereupon Volumnius took Dardanus, Brutus' servant, with him, to see what it was: and, returning straight again, asked if there

64

were any water left. Brutus, smiling gently, told them all was drunk; "but they shall bring you some more." Thereupon he sent him again that went for water before, who was in great danger of being taken by the enemies, and hardly escaped, being sore hurt. Furthermore, Brutus thought that there was no great number of men slain in battle, and, to know the truth of it, there was one called **Statilius**, that promised to go through his enemies (for otherwise it was impossible to go see their camp), and from thence if all were well, that he would lift up a torch light in the air, and then return again with speed to him. The torch light was lifted up as he had promised, for Statilius went thither. Now Brutus seeing Statilius tarry long after that, and that he came not again, he said: "If Statilius be alive, he will come again." But his evil fortune was such that, as he came back, he lighted in his enemies' hands, and was slain.

Part Two

[The historian Appian states that, early next morning, Brutus returned to his troops. When he asked his officers if they would attempt breaking through enemy lines, they replied only that he should look out for himself; and it was after this that he ran on his sword. Plutarch says that this took place while Brutus was still a fugitive in the hills.]

Now, the night being far spent, Brutus as he sat bowed towards **Clitus**, one of his men, and told him somewhat in his ear: the other answered him not, but fell a-weeping. Thereupon he drew aside his armour-bearer Dardanus, and said somewhat also to him: at length he came to Volumnius, and prayed him that he would help him to put his hand to his sword, to thrust it in him to kill him. Volumnius denied his request, and so did many others: and amongst the rest, one of them said, there was no tarrying for them there, but that they must needs fly. Then Brutus rising up, "We must fly indeed," said he, "but it must be with our hands, not with our feet." Then taking every man by the hand, he said these words unto them with a cheerful countenance:

> "It rejoiceth my heart that not one of my friends
> hath failed me at my need, and I do not complain of
> my fortune, but only for my country's sake: for, as
> for me, I think myself happier than they that have

overcome, considering that I leave a perpetual fame of our courage and manhood, the which our enemies the conquerors shall never attain unto by force nor money; no more than they could hinder **posterity** from believing and saying that, being unjust and wicked men, they had destroyed the just and the good, and usurped a power to which they had no right."

Having said so, he prayed every man to shift for themselves, and then he went a little aside with two or three only, among the which **Strato** was one. He came as near to him as he could, and taking his sword by the hilts with both his hands, and falling down upon the point of it, ran himself through. Others say that, not he, but Strato (at his request) held the sword in his hand, and turned his head aside, and that Brutus fell down upon it: and so ran himself through, and died presently.

Messalla, that had been Brutus' great friend, became afterwards Octavius Caesar's friend. So, shortly after, Caesar being at good leisure, he brought Strato, Brutus' friend, unto him, and weeping, said: "Caesar, behold, here is he that did the last service to my Brutus." Caesar welcomed him at that time, and afterwards he did him as faithful service in all his affairs, as any Grecian else he had about him, until the **Battle of Actium**.

It is reported also, that this friend Messalla himself answered Caesar one day, when he gave him great praise before his face, that he had fought valiantly, and with great affection for him, at the Battle of Actium, (notwithstanding that he had been his cruel enemy before, at the Battle of Philippi, for Brutus' sake): "I ever loved," said he, "to take the best and justest part."

Now, Antony having found Brutus' body, he caused it to be wrapped up in one of the richest **mantles** he had. Afterwards also, Antony understanding that this mantle was stolen, he put the thief to death that had stolen it, and sent the ashes of his body unto his mother.

And for Porcia, Brutus' wife, Nicolaus the philosopher and Valerius Maximus do write that she determined to kill herself, choosing to die rather than to languish in pain.

Narration and Discussion

In Shakespeare's *Julius Caesar*, Mark Antony called Brutus "the noblest Roman of them all." Do you agree that Brutus was a hero? What are the things you admire most about him? What do you not admire?

Why did Brutus call himself "happier" (or more fortunate) than those that won the battle?

For older students: In **Lesson One**, Plutarch said that Brutus "framed his manners of life by the rules of virtue and study of philosophy." How did that shape the outcome of his story?

For Christian students in particular: Compare this somber scene to the story of Jesus Christ in the garden of Gethsemane. Both men knew they would soon be facing death. Are there any similarities in the stories? What are the greatest differences? Pay particular attention to the things they said.

Examination Questions

Younger Students:

1. a) Why did Caesar honour and esteem Brutus? b) Give an account of the meeting of Brutus and Cassius at Sardis, or at Smyrna.

2. (Alternative) How did Lucilius save the life of Brutus?

Older Students:

1. Give an account of the way in which Brutus and Cassius prepared for the battle of the Philippian Fields.

2. (Alternative) "Brutus…tasted of the benefit of Caesar's favour…" Give instances. OR, How did Favonius end the quarrel between Brutus and Cassius at Sardis? What led to it? Tell the whole story.

3. (For high school) Compare and contrast the characters of Cassius and Brutus, giving illustrations. OR "He was right made and framed unto virtue." Give instances to show how Plutarch justifies this estimate of treatment of the pirates.

Pericles

(ca. 495-429 B.C.)

"We find Plutarch's Lives exceedingly inspiring.
These are read by the teacher... and narrated with
great spirit by the children. They learn to answer
such questions as,—'In what ways did Pericles make
Athens beautiful? How did he persuade the people
to help him?' And we may hope that the idea is
engendered of preserving and increasing the beauty
of their own neighbourhood without the staleness
which comes of much exhortation." Charlotte
Mason, *Philosophy of Education*

Pericles is considered the greatest statesman Athens ever had, although
he was not the king, the president, or even the mayor of the city.

The time period covered in this story is the life of Pericles, but
especially the fifty years from 480 to 430 B.C., the "Golden Age of
Athens." During this time, the city-state of Athens was at its political
and cultural peak. It was more or less at peace after the worst battles
of the Persian War; it had a strong navy, created during that war; it had
also become the leader of a group of states called the Delian League.

The people of Athens believed that everyone could and should contribute to the life of the city: because the city wasn't where they lived, *they* were the city, in much the same way as Christians who say that the church is the body of believers. The goddess **Athena** (also called **Pallas Athena**) for whom Athens was named, wore armour and was called the goddess of victory, but she was also in charge of wisdom and the arts. There is a legend that when Athena's temple was destroyed in the Persian War, a tiny olive shoot (the olive was her special tree) sprouted on the temple site as a sign of hope and rebirth. The Athenians put their faith in that sign, and their efforts into building something both beautiful and strong in her honour.

The Government of Athens

Athens had a system of **democratic** government (government "by the people") which was unusual at that time. It was ruled by an assembly of all the male citizens (excluding slaves and foreigners), which was intended to give equal chances for all to be heard. There were ways, however, for some men to become more powerful than others, and becoming a general in the army was one of those ways. This is the position that Pericles held for many years. There was also a ruling council or court), called the **Areopagus**, similar to the Roman Senate; this changed in power and duties over the years. In Pericles' time it seems to have been responsible only for hearing murder trials.

What was Attica?

Attica was the name for the region of Greece which included the city-state of **Athens**. The word **Attic** or **Attican** is sometimes used to describe aspects of Athenian life and culture, such as the "Attic dialect." Attica was bordered by the **Aegean Sea** to the east, **Boeotia** to the north, and **Megara** to the west.

Looking at the Map

Greece is divided in two by the **Isthmus of Corinth**. The southern section, containing **Sparta** or **Lacedaemonia**, is called the

Peloponnesus. The Athenians did not get along very well with the cities in the Peloponnesus, particularly Sparta and Corinth.

The Timeline: Wars and More Wars

In each Plutarch study, I try to include notes about the timeline of events (**Historic Occasions**) that I think will be helpful. Putting dates together for this study has been one of the hardest yet, as my usual sources suggested quite different years for some events. In some cases, such as the end of a war, historians may still be debating when and how it happened. There is also the problem that Plutarch, drawing on his own sources, had to piece together the story himself; and he sometimes moves forward and then backward in the telling. However, specific dates, for this study, are less important than the big events.

It might help to make a timeline or chart showing the years 500-400 B.C. With one colour, shade in or circle the years 499-449, the span of the Greco-Persian Wars. With a second colour, mark the years 460-445, the First Peloponnesian War (it will overlap the first). The "Thirty Years' Peace" between Athens and Sparta began in 446/445, although it did not last that long.

With a third colour, mark 431-404, the Second Peloponnesian War (sometimes just called the Peloponnesian War). Note how few years of that century there were in which Athens was not involved in a major conflict.

The Parthenon was built between 447 and 438, although some work on the buildings continued until 432.

Mark the birth of Pericles in approximately 495, and his death in 429. You might also mark the last fifteen years of his life, in which, according to Plutarch, he was the undisputed leader in Athens.

Helpful Resources

A supplementary book you may find helpful is *Temple on a Hill: The Building of the Parthenon*, by Anne Rockwell. It was published in 1969 but may still be available in libraries and can also be accessed online.

Older students may find it interesting to compare Plutarch's version with Thucydides' history of the times, *The Peloponnesian Wars*.

Top Ten Vocabulary Terms in the *Life of Pericles*

If you recognize these words, you are well on your way to mastering Plutarch's vocabulary for this *Life*. They will not be repeated in the lessons.

1. **barbarians:** foreigners, but especially (in this case) the Persians

2. **commonwealth:** in this case, Athens and its satellites or colonies

3. **distemper:** This word is used now mainly for a disease afflicting animals; however, it means any disorder. It is used more than once in this *Life* to describe various group and individual troubles.

4. **factions:** groups divided by disagreement

5. **marketplace:** Like the Roman Forum, the *Agora* in Athens was an public place where business was done and speeches were made.

6. **mean:** low-ranking, poor

7. **oration:** speech

8. ***Ostracismon:*** or Ostracism. This was a banishment, by the votes of the people, of those who threatened to become too powerful.

9. **pulpit for narrations:** platform or other place where public speeches were made

10. **waste:** destroy, ruin

Lesson One

Introduction

Often we admire things that are achieved or created, says Plutarch. However, sometimes we can admire the product without feeling much esteem for the maker. For instance, in Plutarch's own time (not necessarily that of Pericles), music was enjoyed, and musicians were somewhat admired…but it wasn't a career or even a pastime to which he thought high-minded people should spend their energies. In contrast, he says, acts of virtue "can so affect men's minds as to create at once both admiration of the things done and desire to imitate the doers of them." That is his reason for writing biographies: to celebrate the deeds, and to inspire imitation of virtue.

A warning to readers: you may find this first lesson somewhat…abstruse. We begin with the shape of Pericles' head; and then move on to a teacher who seems to have taught him philosophy and political science under cover of music lessons (not unlike Dr. Cornelius in *Prince Caspian*). That first taste of deep thinking awakened his appetite, and moved him on to the heavyweight philosophers of his time, such as Zeno and Anaxagoras. (Anaxagoras reappears later in the story.)

And if anyone thinks philosophy isn't practical, the lesson ends with an example of how Pericles dealt with bullies.

Vocabulary

> **virtue:** We usually use this word to mean moral excellence, but in classical times it also meant "valour," or heroism, courage, and what used to be called "manliness." See the **Discussion Questions**.

> **mean occupation:** menial job

> **affection:** or desire

> **Attican:** see introductory notes

> **sophist:** In ancient Greece, sophists were like "professors," often masters of one field of knowledge.

out of policy: out of caution

natural philosophy: science

hearer: student

People

Damon: Damon was a known expert in music; his other activities aren't as clear. It is possible that historians confused him with his father (who had more political involvements).

Zeno: a famous philosopher and member of the Eleatic school of philosophy founded by **Parmenides**. He lived from about 495 to 430 B.C. We know about his teachings (including his paradoxes) because they are described by philosophers such as Aristotle.

Parmenides: a philosopher who was most active in about 475 B.C.; an explorer of important (and difficult to explain) areas of thought such as metaphysics and ontology. He believed in the impossibility of change ("What exists is now, all at once, one and continuous").

Anaxagoras: A philosopher who lived in Athens for many years. He was interested in all kinds of scientific phenomena, such as the reasons for eclipses. He also taught that all things were formed and existed out of a force of pure reason, called *Nous* in Greek, which is where he got his nickname. In Plato's writings, Socrates says that when he was young, "I eagerly acquired Anaxagoras' books and read them as quickly as I could."

Historic Occasions

(Please see the introduction to this study for an important note about the timeline of Pericles' life.)

ca. 510 B.C.: Birth of Anaxagoras

499 B.C.: Official beginning of the Greco-Persian Wars

ca. 495 B.C.: Birth of Pericles

490 B.C.: Battle of Marathon

480 B.C.: Athens led a coalition of Greek allies against Persia, creating the "Athenian empire"

480 B.C.: Battle of Thermopylae

479 B.C.: Battle of Plataea

On the Map

See the introductory notes for this study.

Reading

Prologue

Like as the eye is most delighted with the lightest and freshest colours: even so we must give our minds unto those sights which by looking upon them do draw profit and pleasure unto us. For such effects doth **virtue** bring: that either to hear or read them, they do print in our hearts an earnest love and desire to follow them. But this followeth not in all other things we esteem; neither are we always disposed to desire to do the things we see well done: but contrarily oftentimes, when we like the work, we mislike the workman, as commonly happens in making perfumes and purple colours. For both the one, and the other do please us well: but yet we take perfumers and dyers to be men of a **mean occupation**.

For it followeth not of necessity that, though the work delight, the workman must needs be praised. And so in like case, such things do not profit those which behold them, because they do not move **affection** in the hearts of the beholders to follow them, neither do stir up affection to resemble them, and much less to conform ourselves unto them. But virtue, by the bare statement of its actions, can so affect men's minds as to create at once both admiration of the things done and desire to imitate the doers of them. And this is the reason why methought I should continue still to write on the lives of noble men, and why I made also this tenth book: in the which are contained the *Lives* of Pericles and of Fabius Maximus. For they were both men very like together in many sundry virtues, and specially in courtesy and justice: and for that they could patiently bear the follies of their people, and the companions that were in charge of government with them, they were marvellous profitable members for their country. But if we have sorted them well together, comparing the one with the other: you shall easily judge, that read our writings of their *Lives*.

Part One

Pericles was of the tribe Acamantis, and the township Cholargus, of the noblest birth both on his father's and mother's side. Xanthippus, his father, who defeated the King of Persia's generals in the Battle of Mycale, took to wife Agariste, the grandchild of Clisthenes (who drove out the sons of Pisistratus, and nobly put an end to their tyrannical usurpation).

[omission for length and content]

Pericles was well proportioned in all the parts of his body, saving that his head was somewhat too long and out of proportion to the rest of his body. And this is the only cause why statues and images of him are made with a helmet on his head: because the workmen as it should seem (and so it is most likely) were willing to hide the blemish of his deformity. But the **Attican** poets did call him Schinocephalos, or squill-head, from *schinos*, a squill, or sea-onion.

[omission for length and content]

Part Two

The master that taught him music, most authors are agreed, was **Damon**…but it is not unlikely, being a **sophist**, that he **out of policy** sheltered himself under the profession of music to conceal from people in general his skill in other things; and under this pretense attended Pericles, the young athlete of politics, so to say, as his training master in these exercises.

[omission for length]

Pericles also was a **hearer** of **Zeno** the Eleatic, who treated of **natural**

philosophy in the same manner as **Parmenide**s did, but had also perfected himself in an art of his own for refuting and silencing opponents in argument; as Timon of Phlius describes it:

Also the two-edged tongue of might Zeno, who,

Say what one would, could argue it untrue.

But he that saw most of Pericles, and furnished him most especially with a weight and grandeur of sense, superior to all arts of popularity, and in general gave him his elevation and sublimity of purpose and of character, was **Anaxagoras** of Clazomenae; whom the men of those times called by the name of *Nous*, that is, "mind," or "intelligence," whether in admiration of the great and extraordinary gift he had displayed for the science of nature, or because that he was the first of the philosophers who did not refer the first ordering of the world to fortune or chance, nor to necessity or compulsion, but to a pure, unadulterated intelligence, which in all other existing mixed and compound things acts as a principle of discrimination, and of combination of like with like. For this man, Pericles entertained an extraordinary esteem and admiration; and, filling himself with this lofty, and, as they call it, up-in-the-air sort of thought, he derived hence not merely (as was natural) elevation of purpose and dignity of language, but, besides this, a composure of countenance, and a serenity and calmness in all his movements, which no occurrence whilst he was speaking could disturb; a sustained and even tone of voice; and various other advantages of a similar kind, which produced the greatest effect on his hearers.

But for proof hereof, the report goeth, there was a naughty busy fellow on a time, that a whole day together did nothing but rail upon Pericles in the marketplace, and revile him to his face, with all the villainous words he could use. But Pericles put all up quietly, and gave him not a word again, dispatching in the meantime matters of importance he had in hand, until night came, that he went softly home to his house, shewing no alteration nor semblance of trouble at all, the man still dogging him at the heels, and pelting him all the way with abuse and foul language. And stepping into his house, it being by this time dark, he ordered one of his servants to take a light, and to go along with the man and see him safe home.

Narration and Discussion

What were the things that Anaxagoras taught Pericles? What does the story of the man bothering Pericles show about what he had learned?

What is "virtue?" In classical culture, virtue meant not only moral excellence and goodness (as we use the word now), but it carried a special meaning of *manly* excellence and valour. The word itself refers to the Latin root "vir," meaning *man*. Low-born people, or slaves, or women, were not considered to be "virtuous."
Does the Bible agree or disagree with what he says? (See, for instance, Proverbs 31:4-7; compare that with New Testament passages such as Colossians 3:23-24.)

For older students: What is Plutarch's aim in writing the *Life of Pericles?* A hint: Plutarch criticizes certain things that "do *not* profit those which behold them, because they do *not* move affection in the hearts of the beholders to follow them, *neither* do stir up affection to resemble them, and much *less* to conform ourselves unto them." Try removing all the "not" words.

Creative narration: Early teachers have a great influence on us. Even homeschoolers have often had teachers outside their family who have helped to shape their thinking: people in their faith community, other adult friends, or even authors of books. Write a thank-you letter to someone (real or literary) who taught you something valuable.

Lesson Two

Introduction

We have read about Pericles' early education and the ideas that were sown in him of rhetoric (beautiful and persuasive speech), rational thinking, and wanting to serve his people. Pericles was now in his mid-twenties and had the opportunity to take on a position of high leadership in Athens. Although he was himself an aristocrat and had no real desire to see power given to the lowest classes of people (in his thinking, lower class men make irrational, emotional decisions), he saw that getting support from the masses was his best tactic against the even more aristocratic Cimon.

Vocabulary

gravity: graveness, seriousness. An **exterior of gravity** is an appearance of seriousness.

fashion himself to all companies: get along more easily with people

presumption: to be **presumptuous** is to show too much confidence in one's own worth or abilities

mere counterfeiting might in time…: By acting in a certain way, they might get to like it, and it would eventually become natural to them.

up and down: we would probably say "all over"

lean to the tribe of the poor people: to support the political issues of the lower classes

not popular, nor meanly given: "Popular" means favouring the common people.

glutted: overfilled

People

Cimon: or Kimon. Athenian statesman and general, the subject of Plutarch's *Life of Cimon*

Pisistratus: or Peisistratos, a leader in Athens about a hundred years before Pericles.

Aristides: Athenian statesman Aristides "the Just," subject of Plutarch's *Life of Aristides*

Themistocles: Athenian politician and general, subject of Plutarch's *Life of Themistocles*

Thucydides, the son of Melesias: leader of the "conservative" party; a political rival of Pericles. (See **Lesson Three**.) He is not to be confused with Thucydides the historian.

Archidamus: Archidamus II, who reigned in Sparta from approximately 476 B.C. to 427 B.C.

Historic Occasions

472/471 B.C.: Ostracism of **Themistocles**

470 B.C.: Birth of Socrates

Decade of 470-460: Pericles' entrance into politics

468 B.C.: Death of **Aristides**

Reading

Part One

The poet Ion sayeth that Pericles was a very proud man, and a stately one; and that with his **gravity** and noble mind, there was mingled a certain scorn and contempt of others: and contrarily, he greatly praiseth the civility, humanity, and courtesy of **Cimon**, because he could **fashion himself to all companies**. But Zenon, contrariwise, did counsel all those that said Pericles' gravity was a **presumption** and arrogance, that they should also follow him in his "presumption": inasmuch as this **mere counterfeiting might in time insensibly instill into them a real love and knowledge of those noble qualities**.

[omission for length and content]

Part Two

While Pericles was yet but a young man, the people stood in awe of him, because he somewhat resembled **Pisistratus**; and the most ancient men of the city also were much afraid of his soft voice, his eloquent tongue, and ready utterance, because in those he was Pisistratus **up and down**. Moreover he was very rich and wealthy, and of one of the noblest families of the city, and those were his friends also that carried the only sway and authority in the state: whereupon, fearing least they would banish him with the banishment of *Ostracismon*, he would not meddle with government in any case, although otherwise he shewed himself in wars very valiant and forward, and feared not to venture his person.

But after the time that **Aristides** was dead, that **Themistocles** was driven away, and that Cimon, being ever in service in the wars as general in foreign countries, was a long time out of Greece: then he came to **lean to the tribe of the poor people**, preferring the multitude of the poor commonalty above the small number of nobility and rich men, the which was directly against his nature. For of himself he was **not popular, nor meanly given**: but he did it (as it should seem) to avoid suspicion, that he should pretend to make himself king. And because he saw Cimon was inclined also to take part with the nobility, and that he was singularly beloved and liked by all the better and more distinguished people: he to the contrary inclined himself to the common people, purchasing by this means safety to himself, and authority against Cimon.

So he presently began a new course of life, since he had taken upon him to deal in matters of state: he was never seen to walk in any street but that which led to the marketplace or council-hall. He gave up going to all feasts where he was bidden, and left the entertainment of his friends, their company and familiarity. So that in all his time wherein he governed the commonwealth, which was a long time, he never went out to supper to any of his friends, unless it were that he was once at a feast at his nephew Euryptolemus' marriage: and then he tarried there no longer, but only while the ceremony was a-doing, when they offer wine to the gods, and then immediately rose from table and went his way. For these friendly meetings are very quick to defeat any assumed superiority, and in intimate familiarity an **exterior of gravity** is hard to maintain. Real excellence, indeed, is most recognized when most openly looked into; and in really good men, nothing which meets the eyes of external observers so truly deserves their admiration, as their daily common life does that of their nearer friends. Pericles now to prevent that the people should not be **glutted** with seeing him too oft, nor that they should come much to him: they did see him but at some times, and then he would not talk in every matter, neither came much abroad among them, but reserved himself (as Critolaus said they kept the Salaminian galley at Athens) for matters of great importance.

[omission for length]

Thucydides, the son of Melesias, was one of the noble and distinguished citizens, and had been his greatest opponent; and, when **Archidamus**, the king of the Lacedaemonians, asked him whether he or Pericles were the better wrestler, he made this answer: "When I," said he, "have thrown him and given him a fair fall, by persisting that he had no fall, he gets the better of me, and makes the bystanders, in spite of their own eyes, believe him." Notwithstanding Pericles was ever very grave and wise in speaking. For whenever he went up into the pulpit for orations to speak to the people, he made his prayers unto the gods that nothing might escape his mouth, but that he might consider before whether it would serve the purpose of his matter he treated on.

[omission for length and content]

Narration and Discussion

Why did Pericles avoid social meetings, and begin "reserving himself" for matters of great importance? Compare this to the style of leadership that Jesus showed.

What was Pericles' greatest goal when he spoke in public? How is this still a good rule for speakers (and writers)? (Look up Psalm 19:14.)

In **Part One**, Plutarch quotes Zeno as saying that "…mere counterfeiting might in time insensibly instill into them a real love and knowledge of those noble qualities." In other words, if we decide to act in a certain way (doing what someone brave would do, even if we feel afraid; or treating someone we don't like much with kindness), positive actions may affect ourselves as much as others. Do you agree? Can you think of examples?

Creative narration: Write or act out a conversation between Pericles and a friend, or an interview with a journalist. What might Pericles have to say about his style of leadership?

Lesson Three

Introduction

Plutarch begins this passage by quoting Pericles' critics, who said that under his rule the Athenians were "changed from a sober, thrifty people, that maintained themselves by their own labors, to lovers of expense, intemperance, and license." As you read this passage, look for ways in which Pericles' actions were good for the people of Athens, and ways in which they were not.

Vocabulary

ill brought up: ill-conceived; a bad idea

entertaining the poor: these and the following actions are the things Cimon did (not Pericles)

enclosures and pales: fences marking private land

largess: gifts

chief archon, or lawgiver…: high public positions in Athens

they who had acquitted themselves…: those who had carried out their duties well

contraried: threatened

burdened: accused

confines: borders

inveighing: speaking against something with hostility

company, faction: political party, group of supporters

their estate and dignity was obscured: the nobility had polluted themselves, so to speak, by mixing with the lower classes

garrisons: Literally, troops of soldiers stationed in a town. In this case, the "troops" were simply the colonists, but their increased presence in the countries of Athens' allies seemed like a good, not-too-threatening way to keep a handle on the locals (this, apparently, was not an unfounded worry).

curious: Dryden says "busy, meddling" (i.e. in things they had no business with)

People

Ephialtes: This is one of those names that might go by quickly, but which should be noted even though Plutarch names him here only once. Ephialtes was a politician who worked to *decrease* the power of the **Areopagus** (see introductory notes); he was the opponent of those who wanted power to stay in the hands of a select few. Pericles assisted Ephialtes in the campaign for more "power to the people."

Thucydides (the historian): author of *History of the Peloponnesian War*

Damonides: possibly **Damon** (see **Lesson One**), who was the son of Damonides

Thucydides of the town of Alopecia: Thucydides the politician (see **Lesson Two**)

Historic Occasions

465 B.C.: Cimon, trying to promote co-operation between Athens and Sparta, led troops to Sparta to help put down a rebellion; but Sparta refused Athens' help (although they accepted that of others), and the alliance between Athens and Sparta was broken.

461 B.C.: Assassination of Ephialtes (see note under **People**)

461 B.C.: Cimon ostracized for ten years

460 B.C.: Birth of Thucydides (the historian)

458/457 B.C.: Athens defeated by Sparta at the Battle of Tanagra

451-449/448 B.C.: Greek fleet sent to Cyprus; death of Cimon; official end of the Greco-Persian Wars

On the Map

Tanagra: a town and its surrounding area, north of Athens, in Boeotia.

country of Attica: the region around Athens (see introductory notes)

town of Alopecia: or Alopeke. North calls it a town, but it was more of a subdivision of Athens.

Chersonese: a region of Thrace

Reading

Part One

Now **Thucydides (the historian)** describes the government of the commonwealth under Pericles as an aristocratical government, that went by the name of a democracy. Others say, on the contrary, that by him the common people were first encouraged and led on to such evils as the custom to divide the enemies' lands, won by conquest, among the people; and of the common money to make the people see plays and pastimes, and that appointed them reward for all things. But this custom was **ill brought up**. For the common people that before were contented with little, and got their living painfully with sweat of their brows: became now to be very vain, sumptuous, and riotous, by reason of these things brought up then. The cause of the alteration doth easily appear by those things. For Pericles at his first coming, sought to win the favour of the people, as we have said before, only to get like reputation that Cimon had won.

But coming far short of his wealth and ability to carry out the activities that Cimon did (such as **entertaining the poor**, keeping open house to all comers, clothing poor old people, breaking open besides all **enclosures and pales** through all his lands, that every one might with more liberty come in, and take the fruits thereof at their pleasure); and seeing himself by these great means outgone far in goodwill with the common people, by **Damonides'** counsel he brought in this distribution of the common money, as Aristotle writeth. And having won in a short time the favour and goodwill of the common people, by distribution of the common treasure, which he caused to be divided among them; and in a short time having bought the people over, what with moneys allowed for shows, and for service on juries, and what with other forms of pay and **largess**, he made use of them against the council of Areopagus, of which he himself was no member, as having never been appointed by lot either **chief archon, or lawgiver, or king, or captain**. For from of old these offices were conferred on persons by lot, and **they who had acquitted themselves duly in the discharge of them** were advanced to the court of Areopagus.

Part Two

Pericles now by these means having obtained great credit and authority amongst the common people, he troubled the council of the Areopagites in such sort, that he plucked many matters from their hearing, by **Ephialtes'** help; and in time made Cimon to be banished from Athens, as one that favoured the Lacedaemonians, and **contraried** the commonwealth and authority of the people. And this was in spite of the fact that Cimon was the noblest and richest person of all the city, and one that had won so many glorious victories, and had so replenished Athens with the conquered spoils of their enemies, as we have declared in his *Life*: so great was the authority of Pericles amongst the people.

Now the banishment wherewith Cimon was punished (which they called *Ostracismon*) was limited by the law for ten years; and, in the meantime, the Lacedaemonians being come down with a great army into the country of **Tanagra**, the Athenians sent out their power presently against them. There Cimon, willing to shew the Athenians by his deeds that they had falsely accused him for favouring the Lacedaemonians, did arm himself, and went on his countrymen's side, to fight in the company of his tribe. But Pericles' friends gathered together, and forced Cimon to depart thence as a banished man. And this was the cause that Pericles fought that day more valiantly than ever he did, and he won the honour and name to have done more in the person of himself that day, than any others of all the army. At that battle also, all Cimon's friends, whom Pericles had **burdened** likewise to favour the Lacedaemonians' doings, died every man of them that day.

Then the Athenians repented them much that they had driven Cimon away, and wished he were restored, after they had lost this battle upon the **confines** of the **country of Attica**: because they feared sharp wars would come upon them again at the next spring. Which thing when Pericles perceived, he sought also to further that which the common people desired: wherefore he straight caused a decree to be made that Cimon should be called home again, which was done accordingly.

[omission for length: Cimon's return to Athens, his return to military leadership, and his death in Cyprus; this can be read in the Life of Cimon.*]*

Part Three

Those that took part with the nobility, seeing Pericles was now grown very great, and that he went before all other citizens of Athens, thinking it good to have someone to stick on their side against him, and to lessen thereby somewhat his authority, that he might not come to rule all as he would: they raised up against him **Thucydides of the town of Alopecia**, a grave wise man, and near kinsman of Cimon's. This Thucydides had less skill of wars than Cimon, but understood more about civil government than he, for that he remained most part of his time within the city: where, continually **inveighing** against Pericles in his pulpit for orations to the people, in short time he had stirred up a like **company** against the **faction** of Pericles. For he kept the gentlemen and richer sort (which they call nobility) from mingling with the common people, as they were before, when through the multitude of the commons **their estate and dignity was obscured**, and trodden underfoot. Moreover he did separate them from the common people, and did assemble them all as it were into one body, who came to be of equal power with the other faction.

But the contention between these two groups was as a deep cut, which divided the city wholly. Therefore Pericles giving yet more liberty unto the common people, did all things that might be to please them, ordaining continual plays and games in the city, many feasts, banquets, and open pastimes to entertain the commons with such honest pleasures and devices: and besides all this, he sent yearly an army of threescore galleys unto the wars, into the which he put a great number of poor citizens that took pay of the state for nine months of the year, and thereby they did learn together, and practice to be good seamen.

Furthermore he sent into the **Chersonese** a thousand free men of the city to dwell there, and to divide the lands amongst them; five hundred also into the Isle of Naxos; into the Isle of Andros, two hundred and fifty; into Thrace, a thousand to dwell with the Bisaltes; and other also into Italy, when the city of Sybaris was built again, which afterwards was surnamed the city of the Thurians. All this he did to rid the city of a number of idle people, who through idleness began to be **curious**, and to desire change of things; as also to provide for the necessity of the poor townsmen that had nothing. This served also to intimidate, also, and check their allies from attempting any change, by posting such **garrisons**, as it were, in the midst of them.

Narration and Discussion

How might too much "generosity" by a politician cause problems?

Why was it important that Pericles (good leader that he was) should have at least one major political opponent? How did he respond to the selection of Thucydides?

For older students: Why was it (strangely enough) better for Pericles' political image to allow his old rival Cimon to return to Athens?

Lesson Four

Introduction

In this lesson and the next, we read about the greatest achievement of the Golden Age: Pericles' building and beautification program in Athens, and especially the Parthenon.

A note to teachers: this topic obviously encourages the use of photographs, virtual museum tours, and other media. There have been reconstructions and models of the entire Acropolis, some of which you can find online. But don't overdo it: a few pictures at the beginning, and perhaps a short video at the end, should be enough to give a sense of what was happening. There will also be no shortage of possible creative narration ideas! Choose those that suit the time and materials you have available, and those which will most enhance your own students' learning.

Vocabulary

sumptuous: splendid, rich-looking

looked askance upon: frowned at

cavilled at: complained about

affront: insult

artificers: craftspeople

stuff: materials

Historic Occasions

447 B.C.: Construction began on the Parthenon

On the Map

Isle of Delos: a Greek island which was considered sacred ; the meeting place of the **Delian League**, the gathering of Greek city-states

Reading

But that which delighteth most, and is the greatest ornament unto the city of Athens, which maketh strangers most to wonder, and which alone doth bring sufficient testimony to confirm that which is reported of the ancient power, riches, and great wealth of Greece to be true and not false, are the stately and **sumptuous** buildings which Pericles made to be built in the city of Athens. Yet this was that of all his actions in the government which his enemies most **looked askance upon** and **cavilled at** in the popular assemblies, crying out how that the commonwealth of Athens had lost its reputation and was ill-spoken of abroad for removing the common treasure of the Greeks from the **Isle of Delos** into their own custody; and how that their fairest excuse for so doing, namely, that they took it away for fear the barbarians should seize it, and on purpose to secure it in a safe place, this Pericles had made unavailable, and how that:

> "Greece cannot but resent it as an insufferable
> **affront,** and consider herself to be tyrannized over
> openly, when she sees the treasure, which was
> contributed by her upon a necessity for the war,
> lavished out by us upon our city, to gild her all over,
> and to adorn and set her forth, as it were some vain
> woman, hung round with precious stones and
> figures and temples, which cost a world of money."

Pericles replied to the contrary, and declared unto the Athenians:

> "that they were not bound to make any account of
> this money unto their friends and allies, considering
> that they fought for their safety, and that they kept
> the barbarous people far from Greece, without
> troubling them to set out any one man, horse, or
> ship of theirs, the money only excepted, which is no
> more theirs that paid it, than theirs that received it;
> so they bestow it to that use they received it for. And
> their city being already very well furnished, and
> provided of all things necessary for the wars, it was
> good reason they should employ and bestow the
> surplus of the treasure in things, which in time to
> come (and being thoroughly finished) would make
> their fame eternal."

Moreover he said that,

> "whilst they continue building, they should be
> presently rich, by reason of the diversity of works of
> all sorts, and other things which they should have

need of; and to compass these things the better, and to set them in hand, all manner of **artificers** and workmen (that would labour) should be set a-work. So should all the townsmen and inhabitants of the city receive pay and wages of the common treasure: and the city by this means should be greatly beautified, and much more able to maintain itself. For such as were strong and able men, of body and of age to carry weapons, had pay and entertainment of the commonwealth, which were sent abroad unto the wars: and others that were not meet for wars, as craftsmen, and labourers: he wished also they should have part of the common treasure, but not without earning it."

[omission for length]

For some gained by bringing material such as stones, brass, ivory, gold, ebony, and cypress. Others got to work and fashioned it: as carpenters, gravers, founders, casters of images, masons. Divers hewers of stone, dyers, goldsmiths, joiners working in artificers' ivory, painters, men that set in sundry colours of pieces of stone or wood, and turners. Other gained to bring **stuff**, and to furnish them: as merchants, mariners, and shipmasters, for things they brought them by sea. And by land others got also: as cart makers, carriers, carters, cord makers, saddlers, collar-makers, and pioneers to make ways plain, and miners, and such like. Furthermore, every science and craft, as a captain having soldiers, had also their army of the workmen that served them, labouring truly for their living, who served as apprentices and journeymen under the workmasters: so the work by this means did disperse abroad a common gain to all sorts of people and ages, what occupation or trade soever they had. And thus came the buildings to rise in greatness and sumptuousness, being of excellent workmanship, and for grace and beauty not comparable: because every workman in his science did strive what he could to excel others, to make his work appear greatest in sight, and to be most workmanly done in show.

Narration and Discussion

Compare the description of the building of the Parthenon to the description of Solomon's Temple in 1 Kings 6-8 and 2 Chronicles 3-4. What are the similarities in the descriptions, and what are the differences, especially the reasons for building the two temples?

Pericles' critics said that he had not only wasted money on these buildings, but that he had misused funds entrusted to Athens by other cities, who would not benefit from Athens' new temples and music halls. Explain his response.

For older students and further thought: In **Lesson One**, Plutarch said "…but contrary oftentimes, when we like the work, we mislike the workman, as commonly in making these perfumes and purple colours. For both the one, and the other do please us well: but yet we take perfumers and dyers to be men of a mean occupation." How would you describe current attitudes towards those occupations?

Lesson Five

Introduction

This lesson continues the story of the building of the Parthenon.

Vocabulary

> **Temple of Pallas:** Pallas Athena, or **Athena**, was the patron goddess of Athens (she was called **Minerva** by the Romans). The **Parthenon**, located on the **Acropolis**, is the temple that was dedicated to her.

> **Chapel of Eleusin:** also called the *Telesterion*; a sanctuary in Eleusis devoted to Demeter and Persephone. There is some argument over who built it, which may be why Plutarch mentions it here.

> **Odeon:** or Odeion: a building at the foot of the **Acropolis**, designed for musical contests

distinction: recognition

Panathenaea: or Panathenaic Games. They were held every four years and included religious ceremonies, cultural events, and athletic competitions.

gate and entering…: the *Propylaea*, or gateway to the Acropolis, designed by **Mnesicles**

otherwise called "Of Health": Both the Greek goddess Athena and her Roman counterpart Minerva were believed to have healing powers. The statue referred to here is one named the *Athena Paeconia* or *Paeonia* ("Athena the Healer").

the goddess' image in gold: Phidias' golden statue, the *Athena Parthenos*, was designed to be the focal point of the Parthenon

People

Zeuxis: Have you ever read the story of the painting contest between Zeuxis and Parrhasius? You can find a retelling in *Fifty Famous People* by James Baldwin.

Historic Occasions

438 B.C.: Work completed on the Parthenon

Reading

But the greatest thing to be wondered at was the speed and diligence of all the building. For where every man thought those works were not likely to be finished in many men's lives and ages, and from man to man: they were all done and finished whilst one only governor continued still in credit and authority. And yet they say, that in the same time, as one Agatarchus boasted himself, that he had quickly painted certain beasts: **Zeuxis**, another painter, hearing him, answered:

> "And I contrarily do rejoice, that I am a long time in
> drawing of them. For commonly slight and sudden
> drawing of anything, cannot take deep colours, nor
> give perfect beauty to the work: but length of time,

adding to the painter's diligence and labour in
making of the work, maketh the colours to continue
forever."

For this cause therefore the works Pericles made are more wonderful: because they were perfectly made in so short a time, and have continued so long a season.

[omission for length]

Now the chief surveyor general of all these works was Phidias (but there were many other excellent work masters in every science and occupation). For the **Temple of Pallas**, which is called the **Parthenon** was built by Ictinus, and Callicrates: and the **Chapel of Eleusin** was first founded by Coroebus.

[omission for length]

The **Odeon**, or music-room, which in its interior was full of seats and ranges of pillars, and outside had its roof made to slope and descend from one single point at the top, was constructed, we are told, in imitation of the king of Persia's pavilion; this, likewise, by Pericles' order.

[omission]

Pericles, also eager for **distinction**, then first obtained the decree for a contest in musical skill to be held yearly at the **Panathenaea**; and he himself, being chosen judge, arranged the order and method in which the competitors should sing and play on the flute and on the harp. And both at that time, and at other times also, they sat in this music-room to see and hear all such trials of skill.

Part Two

The **gate and entering into the castle** was made and finished within the space of five years, under the charge of **Mnesicles**, that was master of the works. And whilst these gates were a-building, there happened a wonderful chance, which declared very well that the goddess

Minerva did not mislike the building, but that it pleased her marvellously. For one of the workmen that wrought there fell by mischance from the height of the castle to the ground, which fall did so sore bruise him, and he was so sick with all, that the physicians and surgeons had no hope of his life. Pericles being very sorry for his mischance, the goddess appeared to him in his sleep in the night, and taught him a medicine, with the which he did easily heal the poor bruised man, and that in short time. And this was the occasion why he caused the image of the goddess Minerva (**otherwise called "Of Health"**) to be cast in brass, and set up within the temple of the castle, near unto the altar which was there before, as they say.

But it was Phidias who wrought **the goddess' image in gold**, and he has his name inscribed on the pedestal as the workman of it, and indeed the whole work in a manner was under his charge; and he had, as we have said already, the oversight over all the artists and workmen, through Pericles' friendship for him; and this, indeed, made him much envied, and his patron shamefully slandered with stories.

[omission for content]

But Pericles perceived that the orators of Thucydides' faction, in their common orations, did still cry out upon him that he did vainly waste and consume the common treasure, and that he bestowed upon the works all the whole revenue of the city. One day when the people were assembled together, before them all he asked them if they thought that the cost bestowed were too much. The people answered him, "A great deal too much." "Well," said he then, "the charges shall be mine (if you think good), and none of yours: provided that no man's name be written upon the works, but mine only."

When Pericles had said so, the people cried out aloud, they would none of that (either because that they wondered at the greatness of his mind, or else for that they would not give him the only honour and praise to have done so sumptuous and stately works), but willed him that he should see them ended at the common charges, without sparing for any cost.

Narration and Discussion

How was it that the Parthenon was able to be completed so quickly, but with so impressive a result?

How did Pericles handle criticism that he had spent too much public money on the buildings? Tell the story (or act it out).

For further thought #1: Plutarch says that most quality projects take time (the Parthenon being the exception). Choose one activity you tend to rush through, and deliberately slow it down. Did you enjoy it more, or have a better result? Another way to explore the time that things take is to set a timer, say for brushing your teeth, or making an unrehearsed speech; and to continue the activity for the full amount of time rather than guessing. You might be surprised how long two minutes take!

For further thought #2: However, G.K. Chesterton also said that "anything worth doing is worth doing badly," meaning that it's not only how *well* we do something, but also about the value that some activities have, whether we do them well or not, and whether we win or not. What is something in which you strive for perfection? What is something that you enjoy doing for its own sake, even "badly?"

Lesson Six

Introduction

Pericles was now the captain of a ship full of excited and excitable people. His chief instrument in steering was the power of persuasive speech; which, Plutarch says, he used skillfully and carefully.

Vocabulary

antagonist: opponent; one who is against you

confederacy: group of people

schism: (pronounced sism); a division or gap

populace: the common people

loose, remiss, licentious: uncontrolled, having few moral boundaries (or being willing to ignore the transgressions of others)

modulations: tone of voice, manner of speaking

austerity: strict manner, sternness

expedient: useful, beneficial

preferred: proposed

patrimony, paternal estate: inheritance from one's father

groat: small coin

like a common: a piece of land held "in common" by the people of a village or town, and used for purposes such as the grazing of animals

diversity: difference

contemplative: devoted to the study of spirituality or philosophy

civil: participating in the life of the community, taking part in business dealings, local government etc.

honest: positive, virtuous. Dryden uses the word "noble."

Historic Occasions

444/442 B.C.: Political power struggle in Athens; ostracism of Thucydides

Reading

Part One

At length, coming to a final contest with Thucydides which of the two should ostracize the other out of the country, and having gone through this peril, he threw his **antagonist** out, and broke up the **confederacy**

97

that had been organized against him.

So that now all **schism** and division being at an end, and the city brought to evenness and unity, he got all Athens, and all affairs that pertained to the Athenians, into his own hands: their tributes, their armies, and their galleys, the islands, the sea, and their wide-extended power, partly over other Greeks and partly over barbarians; and all that empire which they possessed, founded and fortified upon subject nations and royal friendships and alliances.

After this he was no longer the same man he had been before, nor as tame and gentle and familiar as formerly with the **populace**, so as readily to yield to their pleasures and to comply with the desires of the multitude, as a steersman shifts with the winds. Quitting that **loose**, **remiss**, and in some cases, **licentious** court of the popular will, he turned those soft and flowery **modulations** to the **austerity** of aristocratical and regal rule. But he yet held still a direct course, and kept himself ever upright without fault, as one that did, said, and counselled that which was most **expedient** for the commonwealth. He many times brought on the people, by persuasions and reasons, to be willing to grant that which he **preferred** unto them; but many times also, he drove them to it by force, and made them against their wills do that which was best for them. He followed the method of a wise physician, who, in a long and changeable disease, doth grant his patient sometimes to take his pleasure of a thing he liketh, but yet after a moderate sort; and another time also he doth give him a sharp or bitter medicine that doth vex him, though it heal him.

For there arising and growing up, as was natural, all manner of distempered feelings among a people which had so vast a command and dominion, he alone, as a great master, knowing how to handle and deal fitly with each one of them, and, in an especial manner, making that use of hopes and fears, as his two chief rudders: with the one to check the career of their confidence at any time; with the other to raise them up and cheer them when under any discouragement. He plainly showed by this that rhetoric, or the art of speaking, is, in Plato's language, the government of the souls of men, and that her chief business is to address the affections and passions, which are, as it were, the strings and keys to the soul, and require a skillful and careful touch to be played on as they should be.

All of which, not the force of his eloquence only brought to pass, as Thucydides (the historian) witnesseth: but the reputation of his life, and the opinion and confidence they had of his great worthiness, because he would not any way be corrupted with gifts, neither had he any covetousness in him.

For, when he had brought his city not only to be great, but exceeding great and wealthy, and had in power and authority exceeded many kings and tyrants, yea even those which by their wills and testaments might have left great possessions to their children: he never for all that increased his father's goods and **patrimony** left him by the value of a **groat** in silver. And yet the historiographer Thucydides doth set forth plainly enough the greatness of his power [*omission for length*]. For after he had prevailed against the politician Thucydides, and had banished him, he yet remained chief above all others for the space of fifteen years. He had therefore attained a regal dignity to command all, which continued as aforesaid, where no other captain's authority endured but one year.

Part Two

Pericles was not altogether idle or careless in looking after his own finances. His **paternal estate**, which of right belonged to him, he so ordered that it might neither through negligence be wasted or lessened, nor yet, being so full of business as he was, cost him any great trouble or time with taking care of it; and put it into such a way of management as he thought to be the most easy for himself, and the most exact. All his yearly products and profits he sold together in a lump, and supplied his household needs afterwards by buying everything that he or his family wanted out of the market.

[*omission for length: how Pericles' tight management of household finances irritated his family members, but nevertheless kept him from going into debt*]

Part Three

But these things were far contrary to Anaxagoras' wisdom. For he, despising the world, and casting his affection on heavenly things, did willingly forsake his house, and suffered all his land to lie fallow and to be grazed by sheep **like a common**.

But (in my opinion) great is the **diversity** between a **contemplative** life and a **civil** life. For the one employeth all his time upon the speculation of good and honest things: and to attain to that, he thinketh he hath no need of any exterior help or instrument. The other applying all his time upon virtue, to the common profit and benefit of men: he thinketh that he needeth riches, as an instrument not only necessary, but also **honest**. As, look upon the example of Pericles: who did relieve many poor people.

However, there is a story that Anaxagoras himself, while Pericles was taken up with public affairs, lay neglected; and that, now being grown old, he wrapped himself up with a resolution to die for want of food; which being by chance brought to Pericles' ear, he was horror-struck, and instantly ran thither, and used all the arguments and entreaties he could to him, lamenting not so much Anaxagoras' condition as his own, should he lose such a counsellor as he had found him to be; and that, upon this, Anaxagoras unfolded his robe, and, showing himself, made answer: "Pericles," said he, "even those who have occasion for a lamp supply it with oil."

Narration and Discussion

"After this he was no longer the same man he had been before." Explain.

Pericles was skilled in rhetoric (persuasive speaking and writing): so much so that he could persuade an entire city to do as he thought best. With another such man in power, this could have caused disaster. What made Pericles stand apart?

Describe Pericles' system of managing his own money and business. Why did he choose to be so rigid and exact with his household and business expenses?

A very old philosophical problem: Which is better: to earn money, and to use it for good purposes, such as helping others; or to leave material things behind so that you can focus on higher matters? Is there a middle position? (Christian students may want to look at Biblical passages relating to riches and money.)

For close reading and careful thought: On a first reading, we may assume that Anaxagoras had become poor, and that the lesson to be drawn is that those who have wealth should help those in need. However, Plutarch seems here to be illustrating his previous point about the value and uses of wealth. Anaxagoras neglected his own lands so that he could concentrate on "contemplation," possibly as a way of pointing his finger at those who, like Pericles, paid such attention to finances that they had little time for philosophy. We also know, from other accounts, that Anaxagoras had been accused of heresy (he said that the sun and the stars were just burning rocks); and his accusers may have included Pericles. By lying down on the street, he was protesting his mistreatment with a hunger strike. It seems that his verbal rebuke may have meant "Stop hounding me about heresy," or possibly, "I was trying to teach you something," rather than "I am dying of neglect." In any case, Pericles seems to have given him the "oil" that he required. (Or was it Pericles who needed oil?)

Lesson Seven

Introduction

This lesson begins with a planned great meeting of Greeks from many places. Plutarch then explains that the meeting never actually took place, but that he thought it worth mentioning just to show "the spirit of the man." The fact that it didn't take place, however, shows something of the changing climate in Athens, and is a first hint that Pericles' plans would not always bear fruit.

Vocabulary

effected: done, completed

crossing the design underhand: conspiring to prevent the gathering

upon no occasion, and to no purpose: without any good reason

tarry time: wait things out; Dryden says "wait and be ruled by time"

journey to the Chersonese: see **Historic Occasions**

People

Tolmides: an Athenian general known for many military successes

Historic Occasions

Note: These events took place before the building of the Parthenon. After this decade of frequent wars, there were several years of peace which allowed the Athenians to focus on city improvements.

454 B.C.: Pericles led battles against the **Sicyonians** and **Acarnanians**

448 B.C.: Athens assisted the Phocians in the "Sacred War"

447 B.C.: Expulsion of the "barbarians" from the Thracian peninsula

447 B.C.: Death of Tolmides at the Battle of Coronea, a battle which lost Boeotia as part of the Athenian empire

446 B.C.: Euboea and Megara revolted against Athens, but Pericles' campaign to quell the uprising was delayed by a threatened invasion of Attica by the Spartans

445 B.C.: Pericles successful in recovering Euboea

On the Map

Euboea: an island near Athens, of military and agricultural importance

Chersonese: The word "Chersonese" meant "peninsula," so there were several places with that name. The Chersonese referred to here was Thracian Chersonese, now called the Gallipoli Peninsula, on the Aegean Sea.

Oeniadae or **Oiniadai:** a town in ancient **Acarnania**, and the people of that town

Reading

Part One

The Lacedaemonians began to show themselves troubled at the growth of the Athenian power. Pericles, on the other hand, to elevate the people's spirit yet more, and to raise them to the thought of great actions, proposed a decree to summon all the Greeks, in what part soever, whether of Europe or Asia, every city, little as well as great, to send their deputies to Athens to a general assembly, or convention, there to consult and advise concerning the Greek temples which the barbarians had burnt down, and the sacrifices which were due from them upon vows they had made to their gods for the safety of Greece when they fought against the barbarians; and also concerning the navigation of the sea, that they might henceforward pass to and fro and trade securely and be at peace among themselves.

[omission for length: the list of cities and states invited to this conference]

Nothing was **effected**, nor did the cities meet by their deputies, as was desired: the Lacedaemonians, as it is said, **crossing the design underhand**, the attempt being disappointed and baffled first in **Peloponnesus**. I thought fit, however, to introduce the mention of it, to show the spirit of the man and the greatness of his thoughts.

Part Two

Furthermore, when Pericles was chosen general in the wars, he was much esteemed because he ever took great regard to the safety of his soldiers. For by his goodwill he would never hazard battle which he saw might fall out doubtful, or in any way dangerous. He did not envy the glory of generals whose rash adventures fortune favoured with brilliant success, however much they were admired by others, nor did he think them worthy of his imitation; but he always used to say to his citizens that, so far as lay in his power, they (those generals) should continue immortal, and live forever.

And when he saw that Tolmides, the son of Tolmaeus (trusting to his former victories, and the praise and commendation of his good service) did prepare **upon no occasion, and to no purpose**, to enter into the country of Boeotia, and that he had procured also a thousand of the lustiest and most valiant men of the city, to be contented to go with him in that journey, over and above the rest of the army he had levied: he went about to turn him from his purpose, and to keep him at home, by many persuasions he used to him before the people's face, and spoke certain words at that time that were remembered long after: "That if he would not believe Pericles' counsel, yet that he would **tarry time** at the least, which is the wisest counsellor of men." These words were prettily liked at that present time. But within few days after, when news was brought that Tolmides himself was slain in a battle he had lost, near unto the city of Coronea, wherein perished also many other honest and valiant men of Athens: his words spoken before did then greatly increase Pericles' reputation and goodwill with the common people, because he was taken for a wise man, and one that loved his citizens.

Part Three

But of all his journeys he made, being general over the army of the Athenians, the **journey to the Chersonese** was best thought of and esteemed, because it fell out to the great benefit and preservation of all the Grecians inhabiting in that country. For besides that he brought thither a thousand citizens of Athens to dwell there (in which doing he strengthened the cities with so many good men), but also by shielding the neck of land (which joins the peninsula to the continent) with bulwarks and forts from sea to sea, he put a stop to the inroads of the Thracians, who lay all about the Chersonese; and closed the door against a continual and grievous war.

Nor was he less admired and talked of abroad for his sailing around the Peloponnesus, having set out from the port of Megara with a hundred galleys. For he not only laid waste the sea coast, as Tolmides had done before; but also, advancing far up into the mainland with the soldiers he had on board, by the terror of his appearance he drove many within their walls; and at Nemea, with main force, routed and raised a trophy over the **Sicyonians**, who stood their ground and joined battle with him. And having taken on board a supply of soldiers into the galleys out of Achaia, then in league with Athens, he crossed with the fleet to the opposite continent, and, sailing along by the mouth of the river Achelous, overran **Acarnania** and shut up the **Oeniadae** within their city walls; and having ravaged and wasted their country, weighed anchor for home with the double advantage of having shown himself formidable to his enemies, and at the same time safe and energetic to his fellow-citizens.

[omission for length: further adventures at that time]

Narration and Discussion

Pericles disliked taking on military adventures without good reason, especially ones that would risk lives. Give examples of this.

Creative narration: Choose an unusual way to answer the question above.

For older students: Pericles said that he respected the bravery of certain military heroes, but that he chose not to imitate them in foolishly risking the lives of soldiers. He made a similar statement on his deathbed (see **Lesson Twelve**). Why was this so important to him?

For further thought: Does Pericles' statement offer us a way to learn from other ancient "heroes" without necessarily imitating their errors?

Lesson Eight

Introduction

As tensions built within and around Greece, Athens struggled to hold onto dependencies that resented its interference. The rebel on this occasion was the Isle of Samos, and the issue was dominion of the sea. Who had better ships? Who had stronger friends? Athens believed its power was superior; but Samos was ready to put up a good fight.

Vocabulary

made a truce: the Thirty Years' Peace

digression: leaving the main story

oligarchical government: government run by a few select people

tract of time: waiting it out

they would bring it to hazard of battle: they were more than ready to fight

made to draw lots: that is, they did this every day during the siege

lighted on the white bean: a method of choosing, similar to getting the short straw

People

Pissuthnes…: or Pissouthnes. A governor (or *satrap*) of the kingdom of Lydia, including the region of Ionia. He was extremely wealthy, and may have been a grandson of Darius the Great.

Melissus of Samos: a philosopher of the same school as Zeno, and the commander of the Samian fleet

Historic Occasions

446/445 B.C.: Thirty Years' Peace declared between Athens and Sparta

440 B.C.: War against Samos

On the Map

Isle of Samos, Samians: Samos is an island in the Aegean Sea. It was known for its vineyards, and it was also the birthplace of Pythagoras.

Isle of Lemnos: an island in the Aegean Sea

Isle of Tragaea: now called Agathonisi. A small island near Patmos.

Reading

Part One

After this, having **made a truce** between the Athenians and Lacedaemonians for thirty years: he proclaimed open wars against those of the **Isle of Samos**, accusing them that, being commanded by the Athenians to pacify the quarrels which they had against the Milesians, they would not obey.

Sidebar

But because some hold opinion that he took upon him this war against Samos for the love of Aspasia: it shall be no great **digression** of our story, to tell you by the way, what manner of woman she was, and what a marvellous gift and power she had, that she could entangle with her love the chiefest rulers and governors at that time of the commonwealth, and that the philosophers themselves did so largely speak and write of her.

First of all, it is certain that she was born in the city of Miletum, and was the daughter of one Axiochus: she gave herself to entertain the greatest persons and chiefest rulers in her time. Some say that Pericles resorted unto her because she was a wise woman, and had great understanding in matters of state and government. For Socrates himself went to see her sometimes with his friends; and other men brought their wives many times with them to hear her talk.

Yet notwithstanding it seemeth most likely that the affection Pericles did bear her grew rather of love, than of any other cause. For he was married unto a kinswoman of his own; but not liking her company, he gave her with her own goodwill and consent unto another, and married Aspasia whom he dearly loved. Forever when he went abroad, and came home again, he saluted her with a kiss.

[omission for content]

Part Two

But to our matter again. Pericles was charged that he made wars against the **Samians**, on the behalf of the Milesians: for these two cities were at wars together, fighting for the city of Priena, but the Samians were the stronger. Now the Athenians commanded them to lay aside their arms, and to come and plead their matter before them, that the right might be decided: but they refused it utterly. Wherefore Pericles went thither and took away their **oligarchical government**; taking for hostages fifty of the chiefest men of the city; and as many children, which he left to be kept in the **Isle of Lemnos**. Some say every one of these hostages offered to give him a talent; and besides those, many others offered him the like, who were anxious not to have a democracy.

Moreover, **Pissuthnes the Persian, lieutenant to the king of Persia**, for the goodwill he bare those of **Samos**, did send Pericles ten thousand crowns to release the hostages. But Pericles never took a penny: and having that done that which he determined at Samos, and established a democracy among them, he returned again to Athens.

Notwithstanding, the Samians rebelled immediately after, having recovered their hostages again, by means of this Pissuthnes that stole them away, and did furnish them also with all their munition of war. Whereupon Pericles returning against them once more, he found them not idle, nor amazed at his coming, but resolutely determined to receive him, and to fight for the dominion of the sea. So there was a great battle fought between them, near the **Isle of Tragaea**. And Pericles won the battle: having, with four and forty sail only, nobly overcome his enemies, which were threescore and ten in number, whereof twenty of them were ships of war.

[omission for length: Pericles put the city of Samos under siege]

Melissus (the son of Ithagenes, a great philosopher) being at that time general of the Samians: he perceiving that few ships were left behind at the siege of the city, and that the captains also that had charge of them were no very expert men of war, he persuaded his citizens to make a sally upon them. Whereupon they fought a battle, and the Samians overcame; the Athenians were taken prisoners, and they sunk many of their ships. Now they being lords again of the sea, did furnish their city with all manner of munition for wars, whereof before they had great want.

[omission for length]

Pericles being advertised of the overthrow of his army, returned presently to the rescue. Melissus went to meet him, and gave him battle: but he was overthrown and driven back into his city, where Pericles walled them in round about the city, desiring victory rather by time and charge, than by danger, and loss of his soldiers. But when he saw that they were weary with **tract of time**, and that **they would bring it to hazard of battle**, and that he could by no means withhold them: he then divided his army into eight companies, whom he **made to draw lots,** and that company that **lighted on the white bean**, they should be quiet and make good cheer, while the other seven fought. And they say that from thence it came, that when any have made good cheer, and taken pleasure abroad, they do yet call it a white day, because of the white bean.

[omission for length]

At the last, at nine months' end the Samians were compelled to yield. So Pericles took the city, and razed their walls to the ground: he brought their ships away, and made them pay a marvellous great tribute, whereof part he received in hand, and the rest payable at a certain time, taking hostages with him for assurance of payment.

But Duris the Samian describes these matters marvellous pitifully, burdening the Athenians, and Pericles himself, with unnatural cruelty: whereof neither Thucydides, nor Ephorus, nor Aristotle himself maketh mention. And sure I cannot believe it is true what is written.

[omission for length and content]

Narration and Discussion

How is it typical of Pericles that he "desired victory rather by time and charge, than by danger?" How did he keep his soldiers from exhausting themselves during the long siege at Samos?

Creative narration: You are a soldier whose company has just drawn the white bean. Make a list of things you plan to do on your "white day."

For older students: Describe Pericles' relationship with Aspasia.

Lesson Nine

Introduction

Pericles attempted to balance military threats to Athens with the survival of his own political career.

Vocabulary

all but in actual hostilities: were very close to war

aid and succour: assistance and support

affront: insult, annoy

angry: because Athens had interfered

supplications: appeals

redress: correcting an unfair situation

ordinance: decree

was in great estimation: was highly respected

enticed: persuaded (in this case, probably bribed)

every whit: every bit

miscarried with the people: made himself unpopular

impeachment: a charge of misconduct or treason against the state

affiance: trust

tenements: land holdings

Historic Occasions

433 B.C.: Battle of Sybota, between Corcyra and Corinth, with Athenian assistance for Corcyra led by **Lacedaemonius**

432 B.C.: Battle of Potidaea, another battle leading towards full-on-war

431 B.C.: Archidamus of Sparta invaded **Attica**; beginning of the **Second Peloponnesian War**

On the Map

Corcyra: A Greek city, an ally of neither Athens or Sparta, but which received aid from Athens during this conflict

Megara, Megarians: A Greek city, allied with Corinth. Pericles' trade embargoes against Megara caused great anger in that region.

Aeginetans: those of **Aegina**, an island in the **Saronic Gulf** (near Corinth), which was considered a rival for power with Athens

Potidaea: a colony founded by Corinth

Reading

Part One

After this was over, the **Peloponnesian War** beginning to break out in full tide, he advised the people to send help to the **Corcyraeans**, who were attacked by the Corinthians; and to secure to themselves an island possessed of great naval resources, since the Peloponnesians were already **all but in actual hostilities** against them.

The people readily consenting to the motion, and voting an **aid and succour** for them, he despatched **Lacedaemonius**, Cimon's son, having only ten ships with him, as it were out of a design to **affront** him; for there was a great kindness and friendship betwixt Cimon's family and the Lacedaemonians. Therefore did Pericles cause Lacedaemonius to have so few ships delivered him, and further, sent him thither against his will, to the end that if he did so notable exploit in this service, that then they might the more justly suspect his goodwill to the Lacedaemonians. But Pericles being blamed for that he sent but ten galleys only, which was but a slender aid for those that had requested them, and a great matter to them that spoke ill of them: he sent thither afterwards a great number of other galleys, which came when the battle was fought.

But the Corinthians were marvellous **angry**, and went and complained to the council of the Lacedaemonians, where they laid open many grievous complaints and accusations against the Athenians, and so did the **Megarians** also: alleging that contrary to common right and the articles of peace sworn to among the Greeks, they had been kept out and driven away from every market and from all ports under the control of the Athenians. The **Aeginetans**, also, professing to be ill-used and treated with violence, made **supplications** in private to the Lacedaemonians for **redress**, though not daring openly to call the Athenians in question.

In the meantime also, the city of **Potidaea**, subject at that time unto the Athenians (and which was built in old time by the Corinthians) did rebel, and was besieged by the Athenians, which did hasten on the wars. Notwithstanding this, ambassadors were first sent unto Athens upon these complaints; and Archidamus, king of the Lacedaemonians, did all that he could to pacify the most part of these quarrels and complaints, attempting to reconcile the friends and allies. So it is very likely that the war would not upon any other grounds of quarrel have fallen upon the Athenians, could they have been prevailed with to repeal the **ordinance** against the Megarians, and to be reconciled with them. Upon which account, since Pericles was the man who mainly opposed the idea of repealing it, and stirred up the people's passions to persist in their contention with the Megarians, he was regarded as the sole cause of the war.

[omission for length and content]

Yet some hold opinion that Pericles did it of a noble mind and judgement, to be constant in that he thought most expedient. For he judged that this commandment of the Lacedaemonians was but a trial, to prove if the Athenians would grant them: and if they yielded to them in that, then they manifestly shewed that they were the weaker. Others, contrarily, say that it was done of a self-will and arrogance, to show his authority and power, and how much he did despise the Lacedaemonians.

Sidebar

But the shrewdest proof of all, that bringeth best authority with it, is reported after this sort. Phidias the image maker (as we have told you before) had undertaken to make the image of Pallas: and being Pericles' friend, **was in great estimation** about him. But that procured him many ill-willers. His enemies **enticed** Menon, one of the workmen that wrought under Phidias; and made him come into the marketplace to pray assurance of the people that he might openly accuse Phidias, for a fault he had committed about Pallas' image. His accusation was heard openly in the marketplace, but no mention was made of any theft at all: because that Phidias (through Pericles' counsel) had from the beginning so laid on the gold upon the image, that it might be taken off, and weighed **every whit**. Whereupon Pericles openly said unto his accusers, "Take off the gold and weigh it."

But the reputation of his works was what brought envy upon Phidias, especially that where he represents the fight of the Amazons upon the goddess' shield; he had introduced a likeness of himself in a bald old man holding up a great stone with both hands, and had put in a very fine representation of Pericles fighting with an Amazon *[omission]*. So Phidias was clapped up in prison, and there died of a sickness, or else of a poison (as some say) which his enemies had prepared for him: and all to bring Pericles into further suspicion, and to give them the more cause to accuse him. But howsoever it was, the people gave Menon his freedom, and set him free; and gave the captains charge they should see him safely kept, and that he took no hurt.

[omission for length and content]

Part Two

[**Omission:** *During a time of zealous public inquisition, Aspasia and Anaxagoras were both accused of heresy.*]

As for Aspasia, Pericles saved her, even for the very pity and compassion the judges took of him, for the tears he shed in making his humble suit for her, all the time he pleaded her case: as Aeschines writeth. But for Anaxagoras, fearing that he could not do so much for him: he sent him out of the city. And finding that in Phidias' case he had **miscarried with the people**, being afraid of **impeachment**, he kindled the war, which hitherto had lingered and smothered, and blew it up into a flame: hoping by that means to disperse and scatter these complaints and charges, and to allay their jealousy; the city usually throwing herself upon him alone, and trusting to his sole conduct, upon the urgency of great affairs and public dangers, by reason of his authority and the sway he bore. These are given out to have been the reasons which induced Pericles not to suffer the people of Athens to yield to the proposals of the Lacedaemonians; but their truth is uncertain.

But the Lacedaemonians knowing well that if they could weed out Pericles, and overthrow him, they might then deal as they would with the Athenians: they commanded them they should purge their city of "the Pericles pollution" (referring to some scandal relating to his mother's family). But this fell out contrary to the hope and expectation of those that were sent to Athens for this purpose. For instead of bringing Pericles into further suspicion and displeasure, the citizens honoured him the more, and had a better **affiance** in him than before, because they saw his enemies did so much fear and hate him.

Wherefore, before King Archidamus entered with the army of the Peloponnesians into the country of Attica, Pericles told the Athenians that if King Archidamus fortuned to waste and destroy all the country about, and should spare his lands and goods for the old love and familiarity that was between them, or rather to give his enemies occasion falsely to accuse him: that from thenceforth, he gave all the lands and **tenements** he had in the country unto the commonwealth.

Narration and Discussion

Tell the story of Phidias. Why was he was accused of theft? How did he clear himself of the charge? Why was he imprisoned anyway?

How did all these attempts to discredit Pericles backfire?

For older students: Why was Pericles so stubborn about Megara? Some historians thought it was such an unimportant matter (and Megara such an unimportant place) that Pericles must have been holding some personal grudge, or otherwise that he was "war-mongering" to distract the public from other issues. Another possibility is that Pericles believed that any such apology or change of policy would damage Athens' powerful image, which was already in danger. If you have a group, you could debate this issue.

Creative narration: "Therefore did Pericles cause Lacedaemonius to have so few ships delivered him…" This might inspire an interesting telephone conversation between the various parties.

Lesson Ten

Introduction

The Spartans (Lacedaemonians) invaded Attica by land, because they had little sea power. Their plan was to force the Athenians to come out from behind the safety of their walls and fight. As we have learned already, Pericles hated risking lives unnecessarily, so he tried another tactic: "harassing" (or damaging) the coast of the Peloponnesus by sea.

It was Pericles' hardest test, both in fighting the enemy and in managing his own people. Some trusted his judgment; others were harder to convince. Not go out and fight? Wasn't that a cowardly thing to do? Could the Athenians have held out and forced the Spartans to leave without any bloodshed?

It might have worked, "had not some divine power crossed human purposes."

Sidebar: Pericles' Funeral Oration

"Any one can discourse to you for ever about the advantages of a brave defense, which you know already. But instead of listening to him I would have you day by day fix your eyes upon the greatness of Athens, until you become filled with the love of her; and when you are impressed by the spectacle of her glory, reflect that this empire has been acquired by men who knew their duty and had the courage to do it, who in the hour of conflict had the fear of dishonor always present to them, and who, if ever they failed in an enterprise, would not allow their virtues to be lost to their country, but freely gave their lives to her as the fairest offering which they could present at her feast."

"Such is the city for whose sake these men nobly fought and died; they could not bear the thought that she might be taken from them; and every one of us who survive should gladly toil on her behalf."

Those who have heard of Pericles' Funeral Oration may wonder where it fits into the story. This famous speech appears in Thucydides' *History of the Peloponnesian War*, but it is not mentioned by Plutarch. According to Thucydides, it was given by Pericles at a public funeral for soldiers, at the end of the first year of the war. Questions about its authenticity are less important here than its theme: focusing on the "glory" of Athens and the need for courageous citizenship. This speech is believed to have inspired Abraham Lincoln's Gettysburg Address.

Vocabulary

burning and spoiling: damaging and probably looting

assemble the people in council: Dryden says "convene the people into an assembly"

cast away: lost

dastardliness: cruelty, wickedness

Satyr-king, instead of swords…: These verses (only the first of which is included here) have been translated quite differently by different English translators. They had both satirical and serious meanings for the original audience; for us, it is enough to know that Pericles' enemies were saying that he was cowardly and no longer able to rule effectively. (Teles was apparently known for cowardice.)

jaded: exhausted, demoralized; "sick and tired"

parted: divided

protracted: stretched out

had not some divine power…: This refers to the Plague of Athens, which began at that time.

People

Cleon: a political rival of Pericles

Hermippus: a writer of plays; it was he who accused Aspasia of heresy.

On the Map

Acharnes: a suburb of Athens

Reading

So it fortuned that the Lacedaemonians, with all their friends and confederates, brought a marvellous army into the country of Attica, under the leading of King Archidamus, **burning and spoiling** all the countries he came alongst. They came unto the town of **Acharnes**, where they encamped, supposing the Athenians would never suffer them to approach so near, but that they would give them battle for the honour and defense of their country, and to show that they were no cowards. But Pericles wisely considered how the danger was too great to hazard battle, where the loss of the city of Athens stood in peril, seeing there were threescore thousand footmen of the Peloponnesians, and of the Boeotians together: for so many was their number in the first voyage they made against the Athenians. And as for those that were very desirous to fight, and to put themselves to any hazard, being mad to see their country thus wasted and destroyed before their eyes, Pericles did comfort and pacify them with these words:

> "That trees being cut and hewn down, did spring
> again in short time; but men being once dead, by no
> possibility could be brought again."

Therefore he never dared **assemble the people in council**, fearing lest he should be enforced by the multitude to do something against his will. But as a wise captain of a ship, when he sees a storm coming on the sea, gives order to make all things safe in the ship, preparing everything ready to defend the storm, according to his art and skill, not harkening to the passengers' fearful cries and pitiful tears, who think themselves **cast away**: even so did Pericles rule all things according to his wisdom: having walled the city substantially about, and set good watch in every corner. He passed not for those that were angry and offended with him; neither would be persuaded by his friends' earnest requests and entreaties; neither cared for his enemies' threats nor accusations against him; nor yet reckoned of all their foolish scoffing songs they sang of him in the city, to his shame and reproach of government, saying that he was a cowardly captain, and that for **dastardliness** he let the enemies take all, and spoil what they would.

Cleon, also, already was among his assailants, making use of the feeling against him as a step to the leadership of the people, as appears in these verses of **Hermippus**:

> Satyr-king, instead of swords,
>
> Will you always handle words?
>
> Very brave indeed we find them,
>
> But a Teles lurks behind them.

All these notwithstanding, Pericles was never moved in anything, but with silence did patiently bear all injuries and scoffings of his enemies; and did send, for all that, a navy of a hundred sail unto Peloponnesus; whither he would not go in person, but stayed behind, to keep the people in quiet until such time as the enemies had raised their camp, and were gone away.

Yet to soothe the common people, **jaded** and distressed with the war, he relieved them with distributions of public moneys, and ordained new divisions of subject land. For having turned out all the people of Aegina, he **parted** the island among the Athenians according to lot. Some comfort, also, and ease in their miseries, they might receive from what their enemies endured. For the fleet, sailing round the Peloponnese, ravaged a great deal of the country, and pillaged and plundered the towns and smaller cities; and by land he himself entered with an army the Megarian country, and made havoc of it all. Whence it is clear that the Peloponnesians, though they did the Athenians much mischief by land, yet suffering as much themselves from them by sea, would not have **protracted** the war to such a length, but would quickly have given it over, as Pericles at first foretold they would, **had not some divine power crossed human purposes**.

Narration and Discussion

How did Pericles manage the people in time of war? Explain how he handled criticism and complaints.

Creative narration: You are a writer in fifth-century Athens. Write verses either criticizing or praising Pericles.

Lesson Eleven

Introduction

The Plague of Athens changed not only the course of the war, but that of the Athenian empire; and much of the blame fell on Pericles. Was it a judgment from God, or the gods? Could it have been prevented?

Vocabulary

> **plague:** An exact medical name for the epidemic has never been agreed upon. Based on descriptions from that time (such as that of Thucydides the historian), plus recently-discovered DNA evidence, it seems to have resembled typhus, typhoid, or some type of viral hemorrhagic fever.

the flower of Athens' youth: the best young people

The sickness having troubled their brains…: Dryden translates this "distempered and afflicted in their souls."

bruited abroad: spread rumours

heart of the summer: not a typo, although "heat of the summer" would mean the same thing

pent: penned up

shrouded: covered over, in the same sense as being covered in fog

fold: place where sheep are kept

ill token: sign of bad luck

master of his galley: captain of his ship

in amaze withal: frozen with fear

the most part of voices: a majority vote

common griefs: public (political) troubles

prodigal and lavish of expense: she liked to spend money

put him in suit: took him to court over it

sophists, master rhetoricians: philosophers (see **Lesson One**)

kinsfolks: relatives

pull down his countenance: to have a sad face. Dryden says, "He did not shrink or give in…nor betray or lower his high spirit and the greatness of his mind under all his misfortunes."

constancy: dependability, steadiness

copious: a great amount

People

Xanthippus, Paralus: sons of Pericles by his first wife

Historic Occasions

430 B.C.: Plague of Athens

On the Map

Epidaurus: The major city of the region called Epidauria, on the
Saronic Gulf. It was believed to be a sacred place of healing.

Reading

Part One

For first of all there came such a sore **plague** among the Athenians,
that it took away **the flower of Athens' youth**, and weakened the force
of the whole city besides. Furthermore, the bodies of them that were
left alive being infected with this disease, their hearts also were so
sharply bent against Pericles that, **the sickness having troubled their
brains,** they fell to flat rebellion against him, as the patient against his
physician, or children against their father, even to the hurting of him
(at the provocation of his enemies). Those enemies **bruited abroad**
that the plague came of no cause else but of the great multitude of the
countrymen that came into the city on heaps, one upon another's neck
in the **heart of the summer,** where they were compelled to lie many
together, smothered up in little tents and cabins, remaining there all
day long, cowering downwards and doing nothing, where before they
lived in the country in a fresh open air, and at liberty. "And of all this,"
said they, "Pericles is the only cause, who, procuring this war, hath
pent and **shrouded** the countrymen together within the walls of a city,
employing them to no manner of use nor service, but keeping them
like sheep in a **fold**, maketh one to poison another with the infection
of their plague sores running upon them, and giving them no leave to
change air, that they might so much as take breath abroad."

Part Two

Pericles, to remedy this, and to do their enemies a little mischief, armed a hundred and fifty ships, and shipped into them a great number of armed footmen and horsemen also. Hereby he put the citizens in good hope, and the enemies in great fear, seeing so great a power. But when he had shipped all his men, and was himself also ready to hoist sail, suddenly there was a great eclipse of the sun, and the day was very dark, so that all the army was stricken with a marvellous fear, as of some dangerous and very **ill token** towards them. Pericles seeing the **master of his galley in amaze withal**, not knowing what to do: cast his cloak over the master's face, and hid his eyes, asking him whether he thought that any hurt or no. The master answered him, he thought it none. Then said Pericles again to him, "There is no difference between this and that, saving that the body which maketh the darkness is greater, than my cloak which hideth thy eyes."

But Pericles hoisting sail notwithstanding, did no notable or special service answerable to so great an army and preparation. For he, laying siege unto the holy city of **Epidaurus**, when every man expected they should have taken it, was compelled to raise his siege for the plague that was so vehement: that it did not only kill the Athenians themselves, but all others also (were they never so few) that came to them, or near their camp.

Wherefore perceiving the Athenians were marvellously offended with him, he did what he could to comfort them, and put them in heart again: but all was in vain, he could not pacify them. For by **the most part of voices**, they deprived him of his charge of general, and condemned him in a marvellous great fine and sum of money, the which those that tell the least do write, that it was the sum of fifteen talents: and those that say more, speak of fifty talents.

Part Three

Now his **common griefs** were soon blown over: for the people did easily let fall their displeasures towards him, as the wasp leaveth her sting behind her with them she hath stung. But his own home and household causes were in very ill case: both for that the plague had taken away many of his friends and kinsmen from him, as also for that he and his house had continued a long time in disgrace.

For Xanthippus (Pericles' son and heir), being a man of a very ill disposition and nature, and having married a young woman very

prodigal and lavish of expense: he grudged much at his father's hardness, who scantly gave him money, and but little at a time. Whereupon he sent on a time to one of his father's friends, in Pericles' name, to pray him to lend him some money, who sent it unto him. But afterwards when the friend came to demand it again, Pericles did not only refuse to pay it him, but further, he **put him in suit**. But this made the young man Xanthippus so angry with his father that he spoke very ill of him in every place where he came; and, in mockery, reported how his father spent his time when he was at home, and the talk he had with the **sophists** and the **master rhetoricians**.

[omission for length: further quarrels between Pericles and his son]

But so it is, this quarrel and hate betwixt the father and the son continued without reconciliation unto the death. For Xanthippus died in the great plague, and Pericles' own sister also; moreover, he lost at that time, by the plague, the greater part of all his friends and **kinsfolks**, and those specially that did him greatest pleasure in governing of the state. But all this did never **pull down his countenance**, nor anything abate the greatness of his mind, what misfortunes soever he had sustained. Neither saw they him weep at any time, nor mourn at the funerals of any of his kinsmen or friends, but at the death of Paralus, his younger son: for the loss of him alone did only melt his heart. Yet he did strive to show his natural **constancy**, and to keep his accustomed modesty. But as he would have put a garland of flowers upon his son's head, sorrow did so pierce his heart when he saw his face, that then he burst out in tears, and shed **copious** tears: which they never saw him do before, all the days of his life.

Narration and Discussion

Proverbs 18:14 says, "The spirit of a man will sustain his infirmity; but a wounded spirit who can bear?" How did this describe the state of the Athenians during the time of plague? Pericles had as much reason to grieve as the others, but Plutarch says, "All this did never pull down his countenance, nor anything abate the greatness of his mind, what misfortunes soever he had sustained." Explain how he may have been able to do this.

Creative narration: What might have Pericles have thought or said about the avalanche of public and personal tragedies? Older students might write this as a dramatic monologue.

Lesson Twelve and Examination Questions

Introduction

How would you like to be remembered by people? Is it always our great achievements that mean most to us, and to others? Although weakened in body and mind, Pericles found enough strength to assert, on his deathbed, what he felt was his one true achievement as the leader of Athens.

Vocabulary

come abroad: come out of one's house

untowardly: untoward; inappropriate, wrong

enrolled: made an official citizen

worn a black gown: worn mourning

choler: anger

demagogues: usually, people who use flattery and make false promises to gain favour; but perhaps in this case it refers to any would-be popular leaders

invidious arbitrary power: power causing widespread resentment because so much of it depended on the wishes of one person

bulwark of public safety: means of protection for the people

mischief and vice: corruption, illegal dealings

weak and low: kept under restraint

attaining incurable height…: becoming so powerful that it would be unstoppable

People

Alcibiades: (450-404 B.C.), the subject of Plutarch's *Life of Alcibiades*. After his father's death at the Battle of Coronea (**Lesson Seven**), Pericles became one of his guardians.

Historic Occasions

429 B.C.: Death of Pericles

428/427 or 424/423 B.C.: Birth of Plato

Reading

The city having made trial of other generals for the conduct of war, and orators for business of state, when they found there was no one who was of weight enough for such a charge, or of authority sufficient to be trusted with so great a command, regretted the loss of him, and invited him again to address and advise them, to reassume the office of general. He, however, lay at home in dejection and mourning; but was persuaded by **Alcibiades** and others of his friends to **come abroad** and show himself to the people; who having, upon his appearance, apologized for their **untowardly** treatment of him, he undertook the public affairs once more.

[Omission for length and content: Pericles, reinstated as governor of Athens, attempted to revoke a law which he had made himself, giving citizenship only to children born of two Athenian parents. This change was now personally important to him since his surviving son (by Aspasia) did not meet that requirement. After discussion, it was agreed to allow Pericles the Younger full citizenship.]

About the time when he son was **enrolled**, it should seem the plague seized Pericles, not with sharp and violent fits, as it did others that had it, but with a dull and lingering distemper, attended with various changes and alterations, slowly, by little and little, wasting the strength of his body, and undermining the noble faculties of his soul. So that Theophrastus, in his *Morals*, when discussing whether men's characters change with their circumstances, and their moral habits, disturbed by the ailings of their bodies, leave aside the rules of virtue, has left it upon record that Pericles, when he was sick, showed one of his friends that came to visit him an amulet or charm that the women had hung about his neck; as much as to say, that he was very sick indeed when he would admit of such a foolery as that was.

In the end, Pericles drawing close to death, the nobility of the city, and such his friends as were left alive, standing about his bed, began to speak of his virtue, and of the great authority he had borne; considering the greatness of his noble acts, and counting the number of the victories he had won (for he had won nine battles as general of the Athenians, and had set up as many tokens and triumphs in honour of his country). They reckoned up among themselves all these matters as if he had not understood them, imagining his senses had been gone. But he, contrarily, being yet of perfect memory, heard all what they had said, and thus he began to speak unto them:

> "That he marvelled why they had so highly praised
> that in him which was common to many other
> captains, and wherein fortune dealt with them in
> equality alike; and all this while they had forgotten
> to speak of the best and most notable thing that was
> in him, which was this: that no Athenian had ever
> **worn a black gown** through his occasion."

And sure so was he a noble and worthy person. For he did not only shew himself merciful and courteous, even in most weighty matters of government, among so envious people and hateful enemies: but he had this judgement also to think, that the most noble acts he did were these, that he never gave himself unto hatred, envy, nor **choler**, to be revenged of his most mortal enemy, without mercy shewed towards him, though he had committed unto him such absolute power and sole government among them.

[omission for length]

The course of public affairs after his death produced a quick and speedy sense of the loss of Pericles. Those who, while he lived, resented his great authority as that which eclipsed themselves, presently after his quitting the stage, making trial of other orators and **demagogues**, readily acknowledged that "there never had been in nature such a disposition as his was, more moderate and reasonable in the height of that state he took upon him, or more grave and impressive in the mildness which he used. And that **invidious arbitrary power**, to which formerly they gave the name of monarchy and tyranny, did then appear to have been the chief **bulwark of public safety**; so great a corruption and such a flood of **mischief and vice** followed which he, by keeping it **weak and low**, had withheld from notice, and had prevented from **attaining incurable height through a licentious impunity**."

Narration and Discussion

Comment on Pericles' last statement to his friends. Is it true that no Athenian ever wore mourning because of Pericles' decisions? If Pericles was wrong, could his statement be caused by his weakened state of mind, or was it truly the thing of which he was most proud?

For older students and further thought: Some people (for instance, the founding fathers of the United States?) believe that power inevitably corrupts and that too much political power in itself is a bad thing. Was Pericles the exception?

Examination Questions

Younger Students:

1. How did Pericles seek to win the favour of the people?

2. (alternative) "In what ways did Pericles make Athens beautiful? How did he persuade the people to help him?"

Older Students:

1. (Middle-school students) Same questions as above.

2. (alternative) "How did Pericles manage the people in time of war lest they should force him to act against his own judgment?"

3. High school: Pericles "gave himself to all matters he had learned of Anaxagoras." What were some of these matters, and how did Pericles make use of them?

Fabius

(c. 280-203 B.C.)

Quintus Fabius Maximus Verrucosus (who later received the additional name Cunctator, or "Delayer") was a general and statesman who held, at one time or another, all the highest offices in Rome including that of dictator. If you have read Plutarch's *Life of Pericles*, you will remember that he was known for his calm temper and love of reason. Fabius, also called Fabius Maximus, had much the same temperament.

This story is unlike many of Plutarch's others, in that he skims over most of Fabius' early career and the first sixty years of his life. (See **Historic Occasions** for **Lesson One**.) It was largely because of that previous record, however, that Fabius was called upon in a time of great crisis.

The Prologue to this Story

Before beginning the life of Fabius, you need to know something about **Hannibal**, and his city, **Carthage**. If you have a copy of V.M. Hillyer's *A Child's History of the World*, the chapters "Picking a Fight" and "The Boot Kicks and Stamps" provides the background information in a few pages. Van Loon's *The Story of Mankind* gives more detail in the chapter "Rome and Carthage." Briefly, Hannibal was the brilliant general of the city of Carthage (in North Africa, across the sea from Sicily); and Carthage was a longtime rival of Rome. Shortly before the opening of this story, he had invaded Italy from the north, over the Alps, with his army and his elephants; he ambushed the Roman forces at the River Trebia (in December 218 B.C.), and slaughtered them again at Lake Trasimene (May 217 B.C.; see **Lesson One**). In desperation, the Romans decided that it was time to elect a dictator, and Quintus Fabius Maximus was the trusted (though aging) choice.

To show how much Hannibal was detested and dreaded by the Romans, there were two Latin sayings about him that became used later as proverbs: "Hannibal (is) before the gates" (which meant that danger was on the way, but people weren't paying enough attention), and "Hannibal (is right) at the gates." Roman adults sometimes used the second one to frighten misbehaving children.

What was the Second Punic War?

From 218-201 B.C., the Romans were at war against Carthage; it was the second of three such wars. *Punicus* was the Latin word for Carthaginian; it referred to their Phoenician origins.

Who was Scipio?

Publius Cornelius Scipio Africanus, now often called **Scipio Africanus**, was born about the time that Fabius first entered politics, and grew up to be the top Roman general at the end of the **Second Punic War**. In Fabius' last years, he was seen as a rival for respect and popularity, particularly because he took an aggressive stand against the Carthaginians, risking more than Fabius considered acceptable. His **surname**, "Africanus," was given to him only after his victories there. For that reason, I have referred to him as Plutarch did: **Cornelius Scipio** or **Scipio**. There are other Scipios mentioned in other *Lives* (such as Metellus Scipio, the father-in-law of Marcus Brutus); but Cornelius Scipio is the only one we are concerned with here.

The Government of the Roman Republic

Social Classes

There were two different types of class divisions in ancient Rome. The first was family-based, between the patricians (the nobility) and the plebeians (common people).

The second type were property- or wealth-based classes such as the *senatores*, the wealthiest citizens, who owned large amounts of land. The next level down, the equestrian class (in North's translation, the knights of Rome), was a "business class," made up of those who could afford horses and who made up the cavalry, or soldiers on horseback, in times of war. Besides the equestrian class, there were three classes of property owners; and then, lowest of all, the proletarii.

Were the *senatores* the same as the senators?

Often, but the two were not identical. Over the centuries, both the size of the Senate and the personal requirements for membership (age, wealth) changed. Some plebeians became senators along with the patricians. Those elected to magistracies (see below) were also included in the Senate.

What was an aedile, a quaestor, a consul?

The elected positions, or magistracies, in Rome were (starting at the bottom): quaestor, aedile, praetor, and consul. (The office of tribune was a separate position, explained below.) There were various numbers of each of these: for example, two consuls were elected each year. Ex-consuls could become censors; and a consul could become dictator if the need (usually a great emergency) arose. In the case of Fabius, he was given the position of dictator without being consul.

Who were the tribunes?

The duty of a non-military tribune (sometimes called a tribune of the plebeians, or plebs; or a "tribune of the people") was to protect the liberties of the common people from any individual or group (such as the nobles) who might take advantage of them or suppress their rights. This position was not part of the junior-senior ranking of magistrates such as quaestor and consul; it was an office voted on by the common people (plebeians), who themselves were bound by oath to protect the tribunes from harm.

Top Vocabulary Terms in the *Life of Fabius*

If you recognize these words, you are well on your way to mastering Plutarch's vocabulary for this *Life*. They will not be repeated in the lessons.

1. **commonwealth:** a general term referring to a country or a city/state (like Rome), and its colonies or associated territories or countries

2. **environ:** surround

3. **impetuous:** moving rapidly and with great force, in an unrestrained or unthinking manner; often refers to someone's temperament

4. **keep:** often means "guard"

5. **oration:** speech

6. **rash:** doing something in haste without considering the consequences

7. **skirmish:** small, unplanned battle

8. **strait:** tight, narrow; a tight, narrow place (such as a narrow pathway or channel of water)

9. **succour:** aid

10. **tarry:** delay, wait; wait for someone or something

Lesson One

Introduction

The Fabia family was part of Rome's noble class. Fabius Maximus had a number of illustrious grandparents and great-grandparents who had been war heroes and consuls. But as a young man, he didn't seem like anyone who would ever set the world on fire. Certainly his boyhood nicknames "Warty" and "Lamb" didn't show that others had a great opinion of his strength and intelligence. However, Plutarch points out that slowness may just mean that someone is too smart to rush into things.

Vocabulary

surname: a Roman surname was an extra name, given after a special event such as a military victory

insensible: without feeling

inuring: toughening, hardening

eloquence: skill in speaking

sententious: full of wisdom and meaning, or (more often) merely attempting to appear so

triumph: to gain victory; but this also refers to the "triumph" or victory parade that Fabius was given

inroad or depredation: encroachment, robbery

corn: grain such as wheat or barley

Mars: the Roman god of war

colleague: Publius Furius Philus, the other consul that year

not seasonable: not the right time

prodigies: extraordinary, supernatural things

forbear: hold back

by tract of time: by delaying

residue: survivors of the battle

intelligence: information

People

his son: Quintus Fabius Maximus. We do not know exactly when or how he died, only that it was sometime between his own consulship in 213 B.C. and the death of his father in 203.

Hannibal: See introductory notes

Gaius Flaminius: consul who was killed at the Battle of Lake Trasimene

Gauls: a tribe which was eventually conquered by Rome

Historic Occasions

There are more than the usual number of events listed here, but most of them are background to the first lesson.

280 B.C.: Birth of Fabius

265 B.C.: Fabius consecrated as an **augur** (a priest concerned with omens)

264-241 B.C.: First Punic War

247 B.C.: Birth of Hannibal

237-235 B.C.: Fabius probably entered politics as a quaestor and aedile

236/235 B.C.: Birth of Cornelius Scipio

233 B.C.: Fabius' first consulship, and his **triumph** for a victory over the Ligurians

232 B.C.: Gaius Flaminius proposed a controversial land reform bill

230 B.C.: Fabius was censor

228 B.C.: Fabius' second consulship

223 B.C.: Battle in Gaul

218 B.C.: Tiberius Sempronius Longus was consul; Second Punic War began

November 218 B.C.: The young soldier Cornelius Scipio saved his father's life at the Battle of Ticinus

December 218 B.C.: Romans defeated at the Battle of the Trebia

May/June 217 B.C.: Consul Gaius Flaminius killed at the Battle of Lake Trasimene

217 B.C.: Fabius appointed dictator

On the Map

If students are not already familiar with ancient Rome, or need some review, they should have the chance to look at a map of the Roman Republic and its surroundings.

River Trebia: or Trebbia; a river in northern Italy

Tuscany: a region of central Italy

Lake Trasimene: or Trasimeno; a lake on the border of Tuscany

Reading

Part One

Fabius (who was fourth in descent from that Fabius Rullus who first brought the honourable **surname** of Maximus into his family), was, by way of personal nickname, called "Verrucosus," from a wart on his upper lip; and in his childhood they in like manner named him "Ovicula," or "The Lamb," on account of his extreme mildness of temper. His slowness in speaking, his long labour and pains in learning, his deliberation in entering into the sports of other children, his easy

135

submission to everybody, as if he had no will of his own, made those who judge superficially of him, the greater number, esteem him **insensible** and stupid; and few only saw that this tardiness proceeded from stability, and discerned the greatness of his mind, and the lion-likeness of his temper.

But Fabius himself, when he was called to serve the commonwealth, did quickly show to the world, that that which they took for dullness in him, was merely his gravity, which never altered for any cause or respect; and that which others judged fearfulness in him, was very wisdom. And where he showed himself not hasty, nor sudden in anything: it was found in him an assured and settled constancy. Living in a great commonwealth, surrounded by many enemies, he saw the wisdom of **inuring** his body (nature's own weapon) to warlike exercises; and he gave himself much to **eloquence** also, as a necessary instrument to persuade soldiers unto reason.

His tongue likewise did agree with his conditions, and manner of life. For his speech had not much of popular ornament, nor empty artifice, but there was in it great weight of sense; it was strong and **sententious**, much after the way of Thucydides. We have yet extant his funeral oration upon the death of **his son**, which he recited before the people.

Fabius was five times chosen consul. In his first consulship, he **triumphed** over the Ligurians (which are people of the mountains, and upon the coast of Genoa); who, being overthrown by him in a great battle, where they had lost many men, they were compelled to go their way, and drove them to take shelter in the Alps, from whence they never after made any **inroad or depredation** upon their neighbours.

Part Two

(In 218 B.C.), **Hannibal** came into Italy. At his first entrance, having gained a great battle near the **River Trebia**, he passed further, and went through **Tuscany**, wasting and destroying all the country as he passed by. This made Rome quake for fear. Besides they saw many signs and tokens, some common unto them, as thundering, lightning, and such other like: but other also more strange, never seen nor heard of before. For it was said that some shields sweated blood; that at

Antium, where they reaped the **corn**, many of the ears were filled with blood; that it had rained red-hot stones; that the Falerians had seen the heavens open and several scrolls falling down, in one of which was plainly written, "**Mars** himself stirs his arms."

But all these signs and wonders had no effect upon the impetuous and fiery temper of the consul **Gaius Flaminius**, whose natural promptness had been much heightened by his recent unexpected victory over the **Gauls**, when he fought them contrary to the order of the senate and the advice of his **colleague**. Fabius, on the other side, thought it **not seasonable** to engage with the enemy; not that he much regarded the **prodigies**, which he thought too strange to be easily understood, though many were alarmed by them. But he, understanding the small number of his enemies, and the lack of money that was among them, gave counsel, and was of opinion they should patiently **forbear** a little, and not to hazard battle against a general whose army had been tried in many encounters, and whose object was a battle; but to send aid to their allies, control the movements of the various subject cities, and, **by tract of time**, to wear out Hannibal's force and power, which was like straw set afire, that straight giveth forth a blaze, and yet hath no substance to hold fire long.

When Fabius had thus said enough to persuade Flaminius, yet it would not sink into Flaminius' head. "For," sayeth he, "I will not tarry until the wars come to Rome's gates; neither will I be brought to fight upon the walls of the city to defend it, and as Camillus did, that fought within the city itself in old time." Whereupon he commanded his captains to set out their bands to the field; and though he himself, leaping on horseback to go out, was no sooner mounted but the beast, without any apparent cause, fell into so violent a bit of trembling and bounding that he cast his rider headlong on the ground, he was in no ways deterred; but proceeded as he had begun, and marched forward up to Hannibal, who was posted near **Lake Trasimene** in Tuscany.

This battle was so fiercely fought on both sides, that notwithstanding there was such a terrible earthquake that some cities were overthrown and turned topsy-turvy, some rivers had their streams turned against their course, and the foot of the mountains were torn asunder, and broken open: yet not one of them that were fighting, heard any such thing at all. Flaminius the consul himself was slain at that battle, after he had done many a valiant act; and many of the worthiest gentlemen and most valiant soldiers of his army lay dead about him, the **residue** being fled. The slaughter was great, for the bodies slain were fifteen thousand, and so many prisoners left alive.

After this overthrow, Hannibal made all the search he could possible to find the body of Flaminius, to bury him honourably, because of his valiantness: but he could never be found amongst the dead bodies, neither was it ever heard what became of it.

Part Three

Now as touching the earlier overthrow at **Trebia**, neither the general that wrote it, nor the messenger that brought the first news to Rome, told the truth of it as it was; but related it as a drawn battle, with equal loss on either side. But on this occasion as soon as Pomponius, the praetor, had the **intelligence**, he caused the people to assemble, and without disguising or dissembling the matter, he told them plainly:
"My lords, we have lost the battle, our army is overthrown, and the consul himself is slain in the field: wherefore consider what you have to do and provide for your safety."

These words spoken to the people, as it had been a boisterous storm of weather that had fallen on them from the sea, to put them in danger, did so terrify the multitude, and trouble the whole city for fear: that they were all in amazement, and knew not what to determine. Yet in the end they all agreed that it stood them upon to have a chief magistrate, called in Latin *dictatura*, that should be a man of courage, and could stoutly use it without sparing or fearing any person. Their choice unanimously fell upon Fabius, whose character seemed equal to the greatness of the office, whose age was so far advanced as to give him experience, without taking from him the vigour of action; his body could execute what his soul designed; and his temper was a happy compound of confidence and cautiousness.

Narration and Discussion

Why did Fabius think it was a bad idea for the Romans to engage Hannibal in battle?

Since Fabius was an augur, is it surprising that he paid so little attention

138

to stories of blood in the grain fields and scrolls falling from the sky?

Creative narration: You are a young reporter assigned to write a story about this man who has just been made dictator. If you can get an interview with Fabius, what questions will you ask him?

Lesson Two

Introduction

Fabius was determined to conduct himself as a rock-solid, unquestioned leader; and he was also determined to prove his theory about Hannibal's limited resources and patience, by holding off from battle as long as possible. When criticized for his seeming cowardice, he had a ready answer.

Vocabulary

bundles of rods and axes: the *fasces*, a Roman symbol of authority

assuage: relieve

sestertius, pl. **sestertii:** at that time, a small silver coin

drachmas, obols: units of Greek currency

extol: praise

adversary: opponent

schoolmaster: or pedagogue; a slave who was employed as a tutor, or who might be responsible for taking a student to and from school and generally supervising him; a more current term might be "babysitter"

jealous: this is meant in a protective sense

prating: babbling

People

Lucius Minucius: commander of the cavalry under Fabius

Marcus Minucius Rufus: consul in 221 B.C.

Historic Occasions

217 through early 216 B.C.: A period during which Fabius was able to avoid open battle with Hannibal

On the Map

Apulia, Campania: These regions of Italy are not named here, but they were sites of action during the war. Campania was divided in its loyalties; the city of Capua, for instance, supported Hannibal.

Reading

Part One

This counsel being confirmed by them all, Fabius was chosen dictator, and he named **Lucius Minucius** general of the horsemen. Then he first required the Senate that they would grant him he might have his horse in the wars: which was not lawful for the dictator, but expressly forbidden by an ancient order. Either because they thought the chiefest force of their army did consist in their footmen, which caused the making of this law: whereby the general should be amongst them in the day of the battle, and in no wise should forsake them; or else because the authority of this magistrate in all other things was so great, that it was in manner after the state of a king; yet all this notwithstanding, they were willing thereunto, and that the dictator should have absolute power over the people.

Fabius at his first coming, because he would show the majesty and dignity of his office, and that every man should be the more obedient and ready at his commandment: when he went abroad, he had four and twenty sergeants before him, carrying the **bundles of rods and axes**. And when one of the consuls came to him, he sent a sergeant to command his bundle of rods that were carried before him to be put down, and all other tokens of dignity to be laid aside: and that he should come and speak with him as a private man.

And first to make a good foundation, and to begin with the service of the gods: he declared unto the people that the loss they had received came through the rashness and willful negligence of their captain, who made no reckoning of the gods nor religion: and not through any default and cowardliness of the soldiers. And for this cause he did persuade them not to be afraid of their enemies, but to appease the wrath of the gods, and to serve and honour them. Not that he made them hereby superstitious, but did confirm their valour with true religion and godliness: and besides he did utterly take away and **assuage** their fear of their enemies, by giving them certain hope and assurance of the aid of the gods.

Afterwards the dictator, before the open assembly of the people, made a solemn vow unto the gods that he would sacrifice all the profits and fruits that should fall the next year, of sheep, of sows, of milk cows, and of goats in all the mountains, rivers, or meadows of Italy. And he would celebrate musical festivities, and show other sights in the honour of the gods; and would bestow upon the same the sum of three hundred three and thirty **sestertii**, and three hundred three and thirty Roman pence, and a third part over. All which sum reduced into Greek money, amounteth to fourscore three thousand, five hundred, and fourscore, and three silver **drachmas**, and two **obols**. Now it were a hard thing to tell the reason why he doth mention this sum so precisely, and why he did divide it by three, unless it were to **extol** the power of the number of three: because it is a perfect number by the nature, and is the first of the odd numbers, which is the beginning of divers numbers, and containeth in itself the first differences, and the first elements and principles of all the numbers united and joined together. So Fabius having brought the people to hope, and trust to have the aid and favour of the gods, made them in the end the better disposed to live well afterwards.

Part Two

Then Fabius hoping after victory, and that the gods would send good luck and prosperity unto men, through their valiantness and wisdom:

did straight set forwards unto Hannibal, not as minded to fight with him, but fully resolved to wear out his strength and power, by delays and tract of time: and to increase his poverty by the prolonged spending of his own money, and to consume the small number of his people with the great number of his soldiers. Fabius camped always in the strong and high places of the mountains, out of all danger of his enemy's horsemen. Still he kept pace with them; when they marched he followed them; when they encamped he did the same, but at such a distance as not to be compelled to an engagement; and always keeping upon the hills, free from the insults of their horse; by which means he gave them no rest, but kept them in a continual alarm.

Thus by delaying, and prolonging the time in this sort: he became disliked of everybody. For every man, both in his own camp and abroad, spoke very ill of him openly; and as for his enemies, they took him for no better than a rank coward; and this opinion prevailed yet more in Hannibal's army. Hannibal was himself the only man who was not deceived, who discerned his skill and detected his tactics, and saw, unless he could be art or force bring him to battle, that the Carthaginians, unable to use the arms in which they were superior, and suffering the continual drain of lives and treasure in which they were inferior, would in the end come to nothing. Thereupon Hannibal began to bethink him, and devise all the stratagems and policies of war he could imagine: and like a cunning wrestler, to seek out all the tricks he could to give his **adversary** the fall. He, at one time, attacked, and sought to distract his attention, tried to draw him off in various directions, and endeavoured in all ways to tempt him from his safe policy.

All this artifice had no effect upon the firm judgment and conviction of the dictator; yet upon the common soldier, and even upon the general of the horse himself, it had too great an operation. Minucius, unseasonably eager for action, bold and confident, humoured the soldiery; and himself contributed to fill them with wild eagerness and empty hopes, which they vented in reproaches upon Fabius, calling him Hannibal's **schoolmaster**; and contrariwise they commended Minucius for a valiant captain and worthy Roman. This made Minucius look high and have a proud opinion of himself, mocking Fabius because he ever lodged on the hills, saying that he seated them there as in a theatre, to see their enemies waste and burn

Italy before their face.

Moreover, he asked Fabius' friends, whether he would in the end lodge his camp in the sky, that he did climb up so high upon mountains, mistrusting the earth: or else that he was so afraid, his enemies would find him out, that he went to hide himself in the clouds. Fabius' friends made report of these jests, and advised him rather to hazard battle, than to bear such reproachful words as were spoken of him. But Fabius answered them:

> "If I should yield to that which you counsel me, I
> should show myself a greater coward than I am
> taken for now, by leaving my determination for fear
> of their mocks and spiteful words. For it is no
> shame for a man to stand fearful, and **jealous** of
> the welfare and safety of his country: but otherwise
> to be afraid of the wagging of every straw, or to
> regard every common **prating**, it is not the part of
> a worthy man of charge, but rather of a base-
> minded person, to seek to please those whom he
> ought to command and govern, because they are but
> fools."

Narration and Discussion

Fabius did not seem to be a person who was overly concerned with personal appearance or gain. Why did he make a point of insisting that he receive special treatment as dictator?

Discuss Fabius' attitude toward religious ceremonies. What was his opinion about the favour of the gods?

For older students: Discuss, orally or in writing, Fabius' response at the end of the passage. (Dryden translates the last section this way: "By such conduct, he makes [himself] the slave of those whose errors it is his business to control.") Do you agree with his viewpoint?

Lesson Three

Introduction

A tiny misunderstanding can destroy a good plan, as Hannibal found out when his army ended up in the wrong place. However, he was a creative and crafty general, and in getting out of this predicament he caused a great deal of trouble for the Romans, and for Fabius especially. (Warning: this story involves cruelty to animals.)

Vocabulary

but mean: poor

drover: one who drives cattle or sheep

left they their soft pace: they stopped moving slowly

finely handled: manipulated, taken advantage of

incense: anger

depressing: putting into a lower position

punctually: quickly

People

Metilius: Marcus Metilius, tribune of the people in 217 B.C.

Historic Occasions

September 217 B.C.: Battle of Ager Falernus (the Falernian Territory)

On the Map

Casinum: a city on the site of present-day Montecassino

Casilinum: a city in Campania

Reading

Part One

An oversight of Hannibal occurred soon after. Desirous to refresh his horse in some good pasture-grounds, and to draw off his army, he ordered his guides to conduct him to the district of **Casinum**. They mistaking his words, and not understanding well what he said because his Italian tongue was **but mean**, took one thing for another, and so brought him and his army to the end of a field near the city of **Casilinum**, through the midst of the which runneth a river which the Romans call Vulturnus. Now the country lying by it, with a valley opening towards the sea, in which the river overflowing forms a quantity of marshlands, with deep banks of sand; and discharges itself into the sea on a very unsafe and rough shore. Hannibal had now fallen, as it were, into the bottom of a sack.

Fabius, who knew the country and was very perfect in all the ways thereabouts, followed him step by step, and stopped his passage, where he should have come out of the valley, with four thousand footmen, which he planted there to keep the strait; and disposed the rest of his army upon the hangings of the hills, in the most apt and fit places all about. Then with his light horsemen he gave a charge upon the rearward of his enemy's battle: which put all Hannibal's army by-and-by out of order, and so there were slain eight hundred of his men. Whereupon Hannibal would have removed his camp thence immediately, and knowing then the fault his guides had made, taking one place for another, and the danger wherein they had brought him: he had them put to death.

Now to force his enemies to come down from the tops of the hills, and to win them from their strength, he saw it was impossible, and out of all hope. Wherefore, perceiving his soldiers both afraid and discouraged, for that they saw themselves hemmed in on all sides, without any order to escape: Hannibal determined to deceive Fabius. He caused straight two thousand oxen to be chosen out of the herd, which they had taken before in their spoils; and tied to their horns light bundles of reeds, and bunches of the dead cuttings of vines; and commanded the **drovers** that had the charge of them, that when they saw any signal or token lifted up in the air in the night, they should then straight set fire on those bundles and bunches, and drive up the beasts to the hills, toward the ways where the enemies lay.

Whilst these things were a-preparing, he, on the other side, ranged his army in order of battle; and when night came, caused them to march fair and softly.

Now these beasts, whilst the fire was but little that burnt upon their horns, went but fair and softly up the hill from the foot of the mountains from whence they were driven. In so much as the herdsmen that were on the top of the mountains, wondered marvellously to see such flames and fires about the homes of so many beasts, as if it had been an army marching in order of battle with lights and torches. But when their horns came to be burnt to the stumps, and that the force of the fire did fry their very flesh: then began the oxen to fight together, and to shake their heads, whereby they did set one another afire. Then **left they their soft pace**, and went no more in order as they did before, but for the extreme pain they felt, began to run here and there in the mountains, carrying fire still about their horns, and in their tails, and setting light as they passed to the trees.

This was a strange sight to look upon, and did much amaze the Romans that kept the passages of the mountains, for they thought they had been men that ran here and there with torches in their hands. Whereupon they were in a marvellous fear and trouble, supposing they had been their enemies that ran thus towards them, to environ them of all sides: so as they dared no more keep the passages which they were commanded, but forsaking the straits, began to flee towards their main and great camp. They were no sooner gone, but the light-armed of Hannibal's men, according to his order, immediately seized the heights; and soon after the whole army, with all the baggage, came up and safely marched through the passes.

Fabius, before the night was over, quickly found out the trick: for some of the oxen that fled here and there fell upon his army. Whereupon, fearing to fall upon some ambush by reason of the dark night, he kept his men in battle array, without stirring, or making any noise.

The next morning by break of day, he began to follow his enemy by the track, and fell upon the tail of the rearward, with whom he skirmished within the straits of the mountains: and so he did distress somewhat Hannibal's army. Hannibal thereupon sent a certain number of Spaniards (very lusty and nimble fellows, that were used to the mountains, and acquainted with climbing upon them), who, coming down, and setting upon the Romans that were heavy armed, slew a great number of them, and left Fabius no longer in condition to follow the enemy.

Part Two

Thereupon the Romans despised Fabius the more, and thought worse of him than they did before: because his pretense and determination was not to be brought to fight with Hannibal, but by wisdom and policy to overthrow him; whereas he himself by Hannibal was **finely handled** and deceived. Hannibal, then, to bring Fabius further in disliking and suspicion with the Romans, commanded his soldiers when they came near any of Fabius' own lands, that they should burn and destroy all round about them, but gave them in charge in no wise to meddle with Fabius' lands, nor anything of his; and did purposely appoint a garrison to see that nothing of Fabius should miscarry, nor yet take hurt. This was straight carried to Rome, which did thereby the more **incense** the people against him. Their tribunes raised a thousand stories against him, chiefly at the instigation of **Metilius**, who, not so much out of hatred to him as out of friendship to Minucius, whose kinsman he was, thought by **depressing** Fabius to raise his friend.

The Senate also were much offended with Fabius for the bargain he made with Hannibal, touching the prisoners taken of either side. For it was articled between them, that they should change prisoners, delivering man for man, or else two hundred and fifty silver drachmas for a man, if the one chanced to have more prisoners than the other. When exchange was made between them, it appeared that Hannibal had left in his hands, of the Roman prisoners, two hundred and forty more than Fabius had to exchange of his. The Senate commanded there should be no money sent to redeem them, and greatly found fault with Fabius for making this accord: because it was neither honourable, nor profitable, for the commonwealth to redeem men that cowardly suffered themselves to be taken prisoners of their enemies.

Fabius understanding it, did patiently bear this displeasure conceived against him by the Senate. Howbeit having no money, and meaning to keep his word, and not wanting to leave the poor citizens prisoners behind him: he sent his son to Rome, with commission to sell land, and to bring him money immediately. This was **punctually** performed by his son, and delivery accordingly made to him of the prisoners, amongst whom many, when they were released, made proposals to repay the money; which Fabius in all cases declined.

Narration and Discussion

The Romans appeared to have the Carthaginian army trapped between the mountains. Why were they not able to win the battle?

How did Fabius raise ransom money for his soldiers who had been taken by the enemy? What does this show about his character?

Creative narration: Imagine a conversation between Metilius and Minucius, discussing "the Fabius problem."

Lesson Four

Introduction

Headstrong and rash, the commander Minucius was everything Fabius hated; yet he was left in charge when Fabius was needed in Rome. He ignored an order to leave the Carthaginians alone, and attacked a few of them. Successfully, in fact; and the story was "made a great deal more than it was," mainly to make Fabius look foolish.

Vocabulary

according to the duty of his office: as an augur (see **Lesson One**)

forage: can mean to go out and look for supplies, but can also mean to plunder or loot

detachment: group of soldiers

apprehended: realized

adversity: difficulties, misfortune

dispatch: hurry up with

appeased: calmed down and satisfied

magistrateal one: Metilius, as tribune, still had a great deal of authority although Fabius was the dictator

seditious: rebellious, treasonous

vexation: annoyance

his subordinate: one below him in authority

People

Diogenes: a Greek philosopher who lived during the time of Alexander the Great

Historic Occasions

217 B.C.: Against orders, Minucius attacked a detachment of Carthaginian soldiers

Reading

Part One

About this time, he was called to Rome by the priests, to assist, **according to the duty of his office**, at certain sacrifices, and was thus forced to leave the command of the army with Minucius; but before he parted, he not only charged him as his commander-in-chief, but besought and entreated him not to come, in his absence, to a battle with Hannibal.

His commands, entreaties, and advice were lost upon Minucius; for his back was no sooner turned but the new general immediately sought occasions to attack the enemy. And notice being brought him that Hannibal had sent out a great party of his army to **forage**, he fell upon a **detachment** of the remainder, driving them to their very camp, with no little terror to the rest, who **apprehended** their breaking in upon them; and when Hannibal had recalled his scattered forces to the camp, he, nevertheless, without any loss, made his retreat, a success which aggravated the boldness and presumption of Minucius, and filled the soldiers with rash confidence.

The news of this "overthrow" went with speed to Rome, and there they made it a great deal more than it was. Fabius, hearing of it, said he was more afraid of Minucius' prosperity than of his own **adversity**. But the common people rejoiced marvellously, and made great show of joy up and down the marketplace. Whereupon **Marcus Metilius**, one of the tribunes, going up into the pulpit, made an oration unto the people, in the which he highly magnified Minucius, and commended his courage; and fell bitterly upon Fabius, accusing him for want not merely of courage, but even of loyalty. Furthermore, he did accuse the nobility and greatest men of Rome, saying: that from the first beginning they had laid a plot to draw these wars out at length, only to destroy the people's power and authority, having brought the whole commonwealth to the state of a monarchy, and into the hands of a private person; who, by his slowness and delays would give Hannibal leisure to plant himself in Italy, and by time give open passage to the Carthaginians, at their pleasure, to send Hannibal a second aid and army, to make a full conquest of all Italy.

Fabius, hearing these words, rose up straight, and spoke to the people, and tarried not about the answering of the accusations the tribune had burdened him withal, but prayed them they would **dispatch** these sacrifices and ceremonies of the gods, that he might speedily return again to the camp, to punish Minucius for breaking his commandment in fighting with the enemy.

These words immediately possessed the people with the belief that Minucius stood in danger of his life. For it was in the power of the dictator to imprison and to put to death; and they feared that Fabius, of a mild temper in general, would be as hard to be **appeased** when once irritated, as he was slow to be provoked. Wherefore every man held their peace for fear, saving only Metilius the tribune. He, having authority by virtue of his office to say what he thought good (for in the time of a dictatorship that **magistrateal one** preserves his authority), boldly applied himself to the people on behalf of Minucius: that they should not suffer him to be made a sacrifice to the enmity of

Fabius, nor permit him to be destroyed, like the son of Manlius Torquatus, who was beheaded by his father for a victory fought and triumphantly won against orders. And he began to persuade them further to take this tyrannical power of the dictatorship from Fabius: and to put their affairs into the hands of him, that would and could tell how to bring them safely to pass.

The people were tickled marvellously with these **seditious** words, but yet they dared not force Fabius to resign his dictatorship, though they bore him great grudge, and were angry with him in their hearts. Howbeit they ordained that Minucius thenceforth should have equal power and authority with the dictator in the wars, a thing that was never seen nor heard of before.

Part Two

Now the Romans imagined that when Fabius should see how they had made Minucius equal in authority with him, it would grieve him to the heart for very anger: but they came short to judge of his nature, for he did not think that their folly should hurt or dishonour him at all. But as wise **Diogenes** answered one that said unto him, "Look, they mock thee": "Tush," (said he) "they mock not me." Meaning thereby, that he took them to be mocked, that were offended with their mocks. Thus Fabius took everything quietly that the people offered him, and did comfort himself with the philosophers' rules and examples: who do maintain that an honest and wise man can no way be injured nor dishonoured. His only **vexation** arose from his fear lest this ill counsel, by supplying opportunities to the diseased military ambition of **his subordinate**, should damage the public cause.

Lest the rashness of Minucius should now at once run headlong into some disaster, he returned back with all privacy and speed to the army; where he found Minucius so elevated with his new dignity, that, a joint authority not contenting him, he required by turns to have the command of the army every other day. But Fabius would not consent to that, but divided the one half of the army between them: thinking it better he should alone command the one half, than the whole army by turns. So he chose for himself the first and third legion, and gave unto Minucius the second and fourth; and divided also between them the aid of their friends.

Narration and Discussion

How did Minucius' success go to his head? Why didn't Fabius have him punished as he could have?

Discuss this sentence: "Fabius... said that what he most feared was Minucius' success." What did he mean?

"An honest and wise man can no way be injured nor dishonoured." Explain.

Creative narration #1: Write Minucius' account of these events. Then write Hannibal's version.

Creative narration #2: You are a) a political cartoonist for the Rome Daily News, or b) an unknown graffiti artist, and you decide to have some fun with recent events. What will you draw or write?

Lesson Five

Introduction

At the next confrontation, known as the Battle of Geronium, Minucius found out that there was a big difference between chasing down one band of foragers, and taking on the whole Carthaginian army.

Vocabulary

contend: compete

a man so favoured by the people: that is, Minucius

serve his turn: work in his favour

fit and commodious: convenient

a good space: for awhile

tempest: storm

Historic Occasions

Summer/Autumn 217 B.C.: Battle of Geronium

On the Map

Geronium: a town in the present-day region of Molise

Reading

Minucius, thus exalted, could not contain himself from boasting of his success in humiliating the high and powerful office of the dictatorship.

Fabius quietly reminded him that it was, in all wisdom, Hannibal, and not Fabius, whom he had to combat; but if he must needs **contend** with his colleague, it had best be in diligence and care for the preservation of Rome, that it might not be said that **a man so favoured by the people** served them worse than he who had been ill-treated and disgraced by them. The young general, despising these admonitions as the false humility of age, immediately removed with his half of the army, and encamped by himself.

Hannibal, hearing of this, sought opportunity to make their discord to **serve his turn.** Now there was a hill between both their camps not very hard to be won, and it was an excellent place to lodge a camp safely in, and was very **fit and commodious** for all things. The fields that were about it did seem afar off to be very plain and even ground, because they had no covert of wood to shadow them; yet were there many ditches and little valleys in them. Hannibal, had he pleased, could easily have possessed himself of this ground; but he had reserved it for a bait, in proper season, to draw the Romans to an engagement. Now that Minucius and Fabius were divided, he thought the opportunity fair for his purpose; and, therefore, having in the night-time lodged a convenient number of his men in these ditches and hollow places, early in the morning he sent forth a small detachment, who, in the sight of Minucius, proceeded to possess themselves of the rising ground.

According to his expectation, Minucius swallowed the bait. He first sent out his light horsemen, and afterwards all his men-at-arms: and lastly perceiving that Hannibal himself came to relieve his men that were upon the hill, he himself marched forward also with all the rest of his army in order of battle, and gave a hot charge upon them that defended the hill, to drive them thence. The fight continued equal **a good space** between them both, until such time as Hannibal saw his enemy come directly within his danger, so that their backs were open to his men, whom before he had laid in ambush: he straight raised the signal he had given them. At that they rushed forth from various quarters, and with loud cries furiously attacked the Romans in the rear. They slew a great number of them, and did put the rest in such a fear and disorder, as it is impossible to express it. Then was Minucius' rash bravery and fond boasts much cooled, when he looked first upon one captain, then upon another, and saw in none of them any courage to tarry by it, but rather that they were all ready to run away. Which if they had done, they would have been cast away, every man: for the Numidians, finding they were the stronger, did disperse themselves all about the plain, killing all stragglers that fled.

Minucius' soldiers being brought to this danger and distress, which Fabius foresaw they would fall into; and having upon this occasion his army ready ranged in order of battle, to see what would become of Minucius, not by report of messengers, but with his own eyes: he got him to a little hill before his camp, where when he saw Minucius and all his men compassed about on every side, and even staggering and ready to flee, and heard besides their cries not like men that had hearts to fight, but as men scared, and ready to flee for fear to save themselves: he clapped his hand on his thigh, and fetched a great sigh, saying to those that were about him, "O Hercules! how Minucius is gone to cast himself away, sooner than I looked for, and later than he desired?" But in speaking these words, he made his ensigns march on in haste, crying out aloud, "O my friends, we must dispatch with speed to succour Minucius: for he is a valiant man of person, and one that loveth the honour of his country. And though with overmuch hardiness he hath ventured too far, and made a fault, thinking to have put the enemies to flight: time serveth not now to accuse him, we will tell him of it hereafter." So he presently cleared the plain of the Numidians; and next fell upon those who were charging the Romans in the rear, cutting down all that made opposition, and obliging the rest to save themselves by a hasty retreat, lest they should be environed as the Romans had been.

Now Hannibal seeing this change, and seeing how Fabius in person, with more courage than his age required, opened his way through the ranks up the hillside, to come to the place where Minucius was: he made the battle to cease, and commanded to sound the retreat, and so drew back his men again into his camp, the Romans being very glad also they might retire with safety. They say Hannibal in his retiring, said merrily to his friends: "Have not I told you, sirs, many a time and oft, of the hanging cloud we saw on the top of the mountains, how it would break out in the end with a **tempest** that would fall upon us?"

Narration and Discussion

Who showed more courage: Fabius or Minucius?

According to Fabius, what is the best sort of ambition to have?

For older students: How did Fabius demonstrate magnanimity?

Creative narration: Use whatever small figures or objects you have to demonstrate how Hannibal lured Minucius into a trap, and how Fabius then came to his rescue.

Lesson Six

Introduction

Fabius had earned the respect of Minucius; but he soon had to struggle again against another commander's "ignorant eagerness."

Vocabulary

stripped: taken away their weapons etc.

standards: flags or other symbols of authority carried by his troops; also called **ensigns**

stake: risk

flower of the Roman youth: those at their best and most active

consume himself: literally, eat himself up; use up all his resources

pikes: spears

it behoveth: sometimes **behooveth**; it is required, it is one's duty

People

Terentius Varro: consul in 216 B.C.; a supporter of Minucius

Aemilius Paulus: or Lucius Aemilius Paullus; consul in 219 and 216 B.C. He was the father of Aemilius Paulus, the subject of one of Plutarch's *Lives*.

Historic Occasions

216 B.C.: Fabius ended his dictatorship

216 B.C.: Aemilius Paulus and Terentius Varro were consuls

Reading

Part One

After this battle, Fabius, having **stripped** those that were left dead in the field, retired again to his own camp, and spoke not an ill word of Minucius. Minucius then being come to his camp, assembled his soldiers and spoke thus to them:

> "My friends, not to err at all, enterprising great matters, it is a thing passing man's nature: but to take warning hereafter, by faults that are past and done, it is the part of a wise and valiant man. For myself, I acknowledge I have no less occasion to praise Fortune, than I have also cause to complain of her. For that which long time could never teach me, I have learned by experience in one little piece

of a day: and that is this: that I am not able to
command, but am myself fitter to be governed and
commanded by another; and that I am but a fool to
stand in mine own conceit, thinking to overcome
those of whom it is more honour for me to confess
myself to be overcome. Therefore I tell you that the
dictator Fabius, henceforth, shall be he who alone
shall command you in all things. And to let him
know that we do all acknowledge the favour which
we have presently received at his hands: I will lead
you to give him thanks, and will myself be the first
man to offer to obey him in all that he shall
command me."

These words being spoken, he commanded his ensign bearers to
follow him, and he himself marched foremost towards Fabius' camp.
When he came thither, he went directly to the dictator's tent: whereat
every man wondered, not knowing his intent. When he came near the
dictator's tent, Fabius went forth to meet him, on which he at once
laid his **standards** at his feet, and said with a loud voice, "O father";
and his soldiers said unto Fabius' soldiers, "O masters."

Afterwards, every man being silent, Minucius began aloud to say
unto him:

"My lord dictator, this day you have won two
victories. The one of Hannibal, whom you have
overcome: the second, of myself your companion,
whom also your wisdom and goodness hath
vanquished. By the one, you have saved our lives:
and by the other, you have wisely taught us. So have
we also been overcome in two sorts: the one by
Hannibal to our shame, and the other by yourself,
to our honour and preservation. And therefore do I
now call you my father, finding no other name more
honourable to call you by, wherewith I might
honour you: acknowledging myself more bound
unto you for the present grace and favour I have
received of you, than unto my natural father that
begat me. For by him only I was begotten: but by
you, mine and all these honest citizens' lives have
been saved."

And having spoken these words, he embraced Fabius: and so did the soldiers also, heartily embrace together, and kiss one another. Thus the joy was great through the whole camp, and one were so glad of another, that the tears trickled down their cheeks for great joy.

Part Two

Not long after, Fabius laid down the dictatorship, and consuls were again created. But when **Terentius Varro**, a man of obscure birth, but very popular and bold, had obtained the consulship, he soon made it appear that by his rashness and ignorance he would **stake** the whole commonwealth by risking battle: because he had cried out in all the assemblies before, that this war would be everlasting, so long as the people did choose any of the Fabians to be their generals; and he boasted openly that the first day he came to see his enemies, he would overthrow them. In giving out these brave words, he assembled such a power that the Romans never saw so great a number together against any enemy that ever they had: for he put into one camp eighty-eight thousand fighting men. This made Fabius and the other Romans, men of great wisdom and judgement, greatly afraid: since if so great a body, and the **flower of the Roman youth**, should be cut off, they could not see any new resource for the safety of Rome.

They addressed themselves, therefore, to the other consul, **Aemilius Paulus**, a man of great experience in war, but unpopular, and fearful also of the people, who once before had condemned him; so that he needed encouragement to resist the fond rashness of his colleague. Fabius told him, if he would profitably serve his country, he must no less oppose Varro's ignorant eagerness than Hannibal's conscious readiness, since both alike conspired to decide the fate of Rome by a battle.

"It is more reasonable," Fabius said to him, "that you should believe me than Varro, in matters relating to Hannibal. I tell you, if you keep Hannibal from battle only for this year, he shall of necessity, if he tarry, **consume himself**, or else for shame be driven to flee with his army. And the rather because, hitherto (though he seem to be lord of the field), never one yet of his enemies came to take his part; and moreover because there remains at this day in his camp not the third part of his army, he brought with him out of his country."

Unto these persuasions, the consul (as it is reported) answered thus:

> "When I look into myself, my lord Fabius, methinks
> my best way were rather to fall upon the enemies'
> **pikes**, than once again to light into the hands and
> voices of our citizens. Therefore, since the estate of
> the commonwealth so requireth it, that **it
> behoveth** a man to do as you have said: I will do
> my best endeavour to show myself a wise captain,
> for your sake only, rather than for all others that
> should advise me to the contrary."

Narration and Discussion

Minucius said, "For that which long time could never teach me, I have learned by experience in one little piece of a day." What had he learned?

Why was it difficult for Fabius to get Paulus to stand up to Varro's loud insistence on fighting? How successful was he?

Why did Aemilius Paulus say that he felt safer falling onto the enemy's spears than into the hands of the Romans?

For further thought: "My friends, not to err at all, enterprising great matters, it is a thing passing man's nature: but to take warning hereafter, by faults that are past and done, it is the part of a wise and valiant man." The philosopher and writer George Santayana said something similar: "Those who cannot remember the past are condemned to repeat it." How might this apply to studies such as Plutarch's *Lives*?

Creative narration: At the end of this passage, we are given a bit of dialogue between Fabius and Aemilius Paulus. Imagine a similar conversation between Minucius and Terentius Varro. What opinions might Minucius have?

Lesson Seven

Introduction

The Romans seemed ready to take on the Carthaginians. But Hannibal, making use of everything from a dust storm to his own weakest men, had moves ready that even the great Roman army didn't expect.

Vocabulary

importunity: persistence

have his day: alternate days of command

Marry!: Indeed! **Yea, marry** means Yes, indeed!

pretty jest: funny joke

wings: the two side portions of an army (the soldiers on the edges)

of such a gore blood: so covered with blood

subsistence: having what they needed to live (such as food)

banditti: outlaws, robbers

opulent: splendid, rich

Historic Occasions

216 B.C.: Battle of Cannae; deaths of Minucius and **Aemilius Paulus**

On the Map

Apulia: the region of southern Italy located in the heel of the "boot"

Cannae: a village in **Apulia**, near the **Aufidus River**

Venusa: now called Venosa, in the region the Romans called Lucania (now Potenza)

Reading

Part One

All the good intentions of Aemilius were defeated by the **importunity** of Varro; whom, when they were both come to the army, nothing would content but a separate command, that each consul should **have his day**; and when his turn came, he posted his army close to Hannibal, at a village called **Cannae**, by the river Aufidus.

It was no sooner day, but he set up the scarlet coat flying over his tent, which was the signal of battle: so that the enemies at the first sight, began to be afraid, to see the boldness of this new-come general, and the great number of soldiers he had also in his host, in comparison of them that were not half so many. Yet Hannibal, of a good courage, commanded every man to arm, and to put themselves in order of battle: and himself in the meantime taking his horseback, followed with a few, galloped up to the top of a little hill not very steep, from whence he might plainly discern all the Romans' camp, and saw how they did range their men in order of battle.

Now one Gisco (a man of like state and nobility as himself) being with him at that time, told him that the enemies seemed afar off to be a marvellous number. But Hannibal, rubbing his forehead, answered him: "Yea," said he, "but there is another thing more to be wondered at than you think." Gisco straight asked him: "What?" "**Marry**!" sayeth he, "this: that of all the great number of soldiers you see yonder, there is not a man of them called Gisco as you are." This merry answer delivered contrary to their expectation that were with him, looking for some great weighty matter, made them all laugh a-good. So down the hill they came laughing aloud, and told this **pretty jest** to all they met as they rode, which straight from one to another ran over all the camp, in so much as Hannibal himself could not hold from laughing.

The Carthaginian soldiers perceiving this, began to be of a good courage, imagining that their general would not be so merrily disposed as to fall a-laughing, being so near danger, if he had not perceived himself a great deal to be the stronger, and that he had good cause also to make no reckoning of his enemies. Furthermore, he showed two stratagems of a skillful captain in the battle. The first was the situation of the place, where he put his men in order of battle, so as they had the wind on their backs: which raging like a burning lightning, raised a sharp dust out of the open sandy valley, and passing over the Carthaginians' squadron, blew full in the Romans' faces with such a violence that they were compelled to turn their faces, and to trouble their own ranks.

The second policy was the form and order of his battle. For he placed on either side of his **wings** the best and most valiant soldiers he had in all his army: and did fill up the midst of his battle with the worst of his men, which he made like a point, and was farther out by a great deal than the two wings of the front of his battle. So he commanded those of the wings, that when the Romans had broken his first front, and followed those that gave back, whereby the midst of his battle should leave a hollow place, and the enemies should come in still increasing within the compass of the two wings: that then they should set upon them on both sides, and charge their flanks immediately, and so enclose them in behind.

And this was cause of a greater slaughter. For when the middle battle began to give back, and to receive the Romans within it, who pursued the other very wholly, Hannibal's battle changed her form: and where at the beginning it was like a point, it became now in the midst like a crescent or half-moon. Then the captains of the chosen bands that lay out in both the wings made their men to turn, some on the left hand, and some on the right, and charged the Romans on the flanks, and behind, where they were all unprotected: so they killed all those that could not save themselves by fleeing, before they were environed.

Part Two

They say also that there fell out another mischief, by misfortune, unto the horsemen of the Romans, and by this occasion. The horse of Aemilius Paulus the consul, being hurt, did throw his master on the ground; whereupon those that were next him did light from their horsebacks to help him. The residue of the horsemen that were a great way behind him, seeing them alight, thought they had been all commanded to alight: hereupon every man forsook their horse, and fought it out afoot. Hannibal, when he saw that, said: "**Yea, marry**, I had rather have them so, than delivered to me bound hand and foot."

Of the two consuls, Varro saved himself by his horse, with a few following him, within the city of **Venusa**. But Paulus, being in the midst of the throng of all the army, his body full of arrows that stuck fast in his wounds, and his heart sore laden with grievous sorrow and anguish to see the overthrow of his men, was set down by a rock, looking for some of his enemies to come and rid him out of his pain. But few could know him, his head and face was **of such a gore blood**: insomuch as his friends and servants also passed by him, and knew him not. And there was but one young gentleman of a noble house, called Cornelius Lentulus, that knew him, and who did his best endeavour to save him. For he lighted afoot presently, and brought him his horse, praying him to get up upon him, to prove if he could save himself for the necessity of his country, which now more than ever had need of a good and wise captain. But Aemilius refused the gentleman's offer and his entreaty, and compelled him to take his horse back again, though the tears ran down his cheeks for pity: and raising himself up to take him by the hand, he said unto him: "I pray you tell Fabius Maximus from me, and witness with me, that Aemilius Paulus even to his last hour hath followed his counsel, and did never swerve from the promise he made him: but that first he was forced to it by Varro, and afterwards by Hannibal."

When he had delivered these words, he bade Lentulus farewell; and running again into the fury of the slaughter, there he died among his slain companions. In this battle it is reported that fifty thousand Romans were slain, four thousand prisoners taken in the field, and ten thousand in the camp of both consuls.

Narration and Discussion

What was the promise that Aemilius Paulus made to Fabius? Why did he refuse to accept the help of his friend?

Who was most to blame for the disaster at the Battle of Cannae?

For further thought: Twice in this passage, people were led (or misled) by the example of others. First, Hannibal's army was spurred on by the sound of their leaders laughing: at the Romans, they assumed. Later, the Roman army, already surrounded, was further confused by one of the generals being thrown from his horse, and other officers dismounting to help him; all the rest of the soldiers dismounted because they thought they were being ordered to fight on foot! Our actions can, inadvertently, either encourage others or be a stumbling-block to them.

Lesson Eight

Introduction

This short lesson shows Fabius at his best and most appreciated: a cool head in a tumultuous time, and a role model for other leaders. Plutarch wrote, "There was not a man that bare any office, but did cast his eye upon Fabius, to know what he should do."

Terentius Varro also makes a brief reappearance here, expecting to be shamed after his defeat at Cannae, but receiving an example of "noble clemency."

Vocabulary

cause that stayed him: reason for his delay

dispersing: scattering

timorous: fearful

countenance: face

feast of Ceres: A seven-day festival held in April, in honour of the goddess Ceres. Among other things, Ceres was one of the patron deities of the "plebs" or common people.

auspicious signs and presages: good omens

Historic Occasions

215 and 214 B.C.: Fabius was consul (see notes below)

164

More Historic Occasions

The chronology of dictators and consuls at this time is a bit complicated, and Plutarch does not cover all of it. Fabius was dictator in 217 B.C. Aemilius Paulus and Terentius Varro were consuls for 216, but one was killed at Cannae and the other was trapped in Venusia. It was decided to make Marcus Junius Pera dictator (and head of the army) in 216, and Tiberius Sempronius Gracchus his "master of the horse." Pera is noted for his policy of recruiting any possible living bodies into the army, including slaves and criminals.

Just to confuse matters more, Marcus Fabius Buteo, as the oldest living ex-censor, was also made dictator in 216, back in Rome, and given the task of replenishing the Senate due to war casualties. Buteo apparently did not like the idea of there being two dictators, and resigned as soon as the vacant seats were filled.

At the elections for 215, Gracchus had been chosen consul, along with Marcus Claudius Marcellus (see more about him in **Lesson Nine**). Marcellus was a replacement for another consul-elect who had been killed in Gaul. However, the patricians (nobles) argued that two plebeians (non-nobles) could not serve as consuls together; so Marcellus resigned (he continued in military leadership as a *proconsul*); and Fabius was chosen instead. Fabius was elected consul once again the next year (214), along with Marcellus, and it was at this point that they acted as the "two chief generals," as described in **Lesson Nine**. Quintus Fabius Maximus, the son of Fabius, was consul in 213, along with Gracchus. Gracchus, who also continued as a general in the army, died during a Carthaginian ambush in 212 B.C.

On the Map

Capua: a city in Campania, 16 miles (25 km) north of Naples

Reading

Part One

The friends of Hannibal earnestly persuaded him to follow up his victory, and pursue the fleeing Romans into the very gates of Rome, assuring him that in five days' time he might sup in their Capitol. A man cannot easily guess what was the **cause that stayed him**, that he went not, unless it was (as I think) some good fortune or favourable god toward the Romans, that withstood him, and made him afraid and glad to retire. Whereupon they say, that one Barcas, a Carthaginian, in anger said, "You know, Hannibal, how to gain a victory, but not how to use it."

Yet it produced a marvellous revolution in his affairs; he, who hitherto had not one town, market, or seaport in his possession; who had nothing for the **subsistence** of his men but what he pillaged from day to day; who had no place of retreat or basis of operation, but was roving, as it were, with a huge troop of **banditti**; now became master of the best provinces and towns of Italy, and of **Capua** itself, next to Rome the most flourishing and **opulent** city; all which came over to him, and submitted to his authority.

It is the saying of Euripides that "a man is in ill case when he must try a friend"; and so neither, it would seem, is a state in a good one when it needs an able general. And so it was with the Romans; the counsels and actions of Fabius, which, before the battle, they had branded as cowardice and fear; now, in the other extreme, they accounted to have been more than human wisdom; as though nothing but rather a heavenly wisdom and influence, that so long foresaw the things to come, which the parties themselves that afterwards felt them, gave little credit unto before.

Upon this occasion, the Romans placed all their hope and trust in Fabius, and they repaired to him for counsel as they would have run unto some temple or altar for sanctuary. His wisdom and counsels, more than anything, preserved them from **dispersing** and deserting their city, as they did when Rome was taken by the Gauls. For where before he seemed to be a coward, and **timorous**, when there was no danger nor misfortune happened: then when every man wept and cried out for sorrow, which could not help, and that all the world was so troubled that there was no order taken for anything, he contrarily went alone up and down the city very modestly, with a bold constant **countenance**, speaking courteously to everyone, and checked the women's lamentations, and the public gatherings of those who wanted thus to vent their sorrows. He caused the senate to meet, he heartened up the magistrates, and was himself as the soul and life of every office. There was not a man that bare any office, but did cast his eye upon Fabius, to know what he should do.

He placed guards at the gates of the city to stop the frightened multitude from fleeing. He moreover did appoint the time and place of mourning, and did command whosoever was disposed to mourn, that he should do it privately in his own house, and to continue only but thirty days. Then he willed all mourning to be left off, and then the whole city should be purified. So the **feast of Ceres** falling about that time, he thought it better to leave off the sacrifices and procession they were wont to keep on Ceres' day: lest the fewness, and the sorrowful countenance of those who should celebrate it, might too much expose to the people the greatness of their loss; besides that, the worship most acceptable to the gods is that which comes from cheerful hearts. But those rites which were proper for appeasing their anger, and procuring **auspicious signs and presages**, were by the direction of the augurs carefully performed.

[omission for content]

Part Two

But herein the great courage and noble clemency of the Romans is marvellously to be noted and regarded. For the consul Terentius Varro returning back to Rome, with the shame of his extreme misfortune and overthrow, that he dared not look upon any man: the Senate notwithstanding, and all the people following them, went to the gates of the city to meet him, and did honorably receive him. Nay, furthermore, those that were the chief magistrates and senators, among whom Fabius was one, when silence was made, they commended Varro much: because he did not despair of the preservation of the commonwealth after so great a calamity, but did return again to the city, to help to reduce things to order, to execute the laws, and aid his fellow-citizens in their prospect of future deliverance.

Narration and Discussion

How did the "bold constancy" of Fabius help the Romans at this time?

Do you think Varro deserved the commendation given to him? Why or why not?

Creative narration: If you are working with a group, have one person play Fabius, and others line up to ask for his help for various situations. Another possibility for drama might be the return of Varro.

Lesson Nine

Introduction

Fabius returned to the battlefield, along with his co-consul Marcellus. This lesson, though, is more about his ability to put out small fires among his own troops.

Vocabulary

the two chief generals: see notes in **Lesson Eight**

buckler: shield

breach: break, damage

eminent: distinguished

sensible of: aware of

more by favour than by desert: more by personal liking than by merit

if you apply yourself…: if you take your problems to anyone else

churlish: rude

clemency: mercy

husbandmen: farmers

must answer for you: must promise that you will remain in the camp

People

(Marcus) Claudius Marcellus: Highly-honoured Roman military leader and five-times consul; subject of Plutarch's *Life of Marcellus*. Noted for his leadership at the Siege of Syracuse (213-213 B.C.), in which Archimedes was killed.

Historic Occasions

214 B.C.: Fabius and Marcellus led the Roman forces against Hannibal

209 B.C.: Fabius' last consulship

208 B.C.: Death of Marcellus

On the Map

Metapontum: an ancient city on the **Gulf of Tarentum**

Marsians: the people of Marsica, in central Italy

Reading

Part One

When word was brought to Rome that Hannibal, after the battle, was gone into other parts of Italy, then they began to be of good cheer again; and sent a new army and generals to the field, among which **the two chief generals** were Fabius Maximus, and **Claudius Marcellus**, both which, by contrary means in manner, won a like glory and reputation. For Marcellus (as we have declared in his *Life*) was a man of action and high spirit, ready and bold with his own hand, and, as Homer describes his warriors, "fierce and delighting in fights." Boldness, enterprise, and daring to match those of Hannibal constituted his tactics and marked his engagements. But Fabius adhered to his former principles, still persuaded that, by following close and not fighting him, Hannibal and his army would at least be tired out and consumed, like a wrestler in too high condition, whose very excess of strength makes him the more likely suddenly to give way and lose it.

Posidonius tells us that the Romans called Marcellus their sword, and Fabius their **buckler**; and that the vigour of the one, mixed with the steadiness of the other, made a happy compound that proved the salvation of Rome. So that Hannibal found by experience that encountering the one, he met with a rapid, impetuous river, which drove him back, and still made some **breach** upon him; and by the other, though silently and quietly passing by him, he was insensibly washed away and consumed; and, at last, was brought to this: that he dreaded Marcellus when he was in motion, and Fabius when he sat still.

Part Two

In preserving the towns and allies from revolt by fair and gentle treatment, and in not using rigour, or showing a suspicion upon every light suggestion, his conduct was remarkable. It is told of him, that he was informed of a certain **Marsian, eminent** for courage and good birth, who had been speaking underhand with some of the soldiers about deserting. Fabius was so far from using severity against him, that he called for him, and told him he was **sensible of** the neglect that had been shown to his merit and good service, which, he said, was a great fault in the commanders who reward **more by favour than by desert**; "but, henceforth, whenever you are aggrieved," said Fabius, "I shall consider it your fault, **if you apply yourself to anyone but to me**"; and when he had so spoken, he bestowed an excellent horse, and other presents upon him; and, from that time forwards, there was not a more faithful and trusty man in the whole army.

For Fabius thought it more fit that hunters, riders of horses, and suchlike as take upon them to tame brute beasts, should sooner make them leave their savage and **churlish** nature by gentle usage and manning of them, than by beating and shackling of them. And so a governor of men should rather correct his soldier by patience, gentleness, and **clemency**: than by rigour, violence, or severity. Otherwise he should handle them more rudely, and sharply, than **husbandmen** do fig trees, olive trees, and wild pomegranates: who by diligent pruning and good handling of them, do alter their hard and wild nature, and cause them in the end to bring forth good figs, olives and pomegranates.

At another time, some of his officers informed him that one of their men was very often absent from his place, and out at night. He asked them what manner of man he was. They answered him all together, that he was a very good soldier, and that they could hardly find out such another, in all their bands as he; and therewithal they told him, of some notable service they had seen him do in person. Whereupon Fabius made a diligent enquiry to know what the cause was, that made him go so oft out of the camp: in the end, he found he was in love with a young woman, and that to go see her, was the cause he did so oft leave his place, and did put his life in so great danger, for that she was so far off. When Fabius understood this, he sent certain soldiers (unknowing to the soldier) to bring the woman he loved, and willed them to hide her in his tent: and then called he the soldier to him, that was a Lucanian born, and taking him aside, said unto him thus: "My friend, it has been told to me, how you have been many nights out of the camp, against the law of arms and order of the Romans, but I understand also that otherwise you are an honest man, and therefore I pardon your past faults, in consideration of your good service; but from henceforth I will place one over you to be your keeper, who should be accountable for your good behaviour." The soldier was blank, when he heard these words. Fabius, with that, caused the woman he was in love with to be brought forth, and delivered her into his hands, saying unto him: "This is the person who **must answer for you**; and by your future behaviour we shall see whether your night rambles were on account of love, or for any other worse design." Thus much we find written concerning this matter.

Narration and Discussion

In earlier battles, the impetuousness of Minucius collided with the only-when-necessary tactics of Fabius. Why did this not seem to be a problem for Fabius and Marcellus?

Choose either the story of the Marsian or the lovesick soldier, and discuss (orally or in writing) why Fabius' tactics were successful. What other solutions might someone else have tried; do you think they would have worked as well? Do these stories of Fabius give you any ideas for dealing with "difficult customers?"

Creative narration: Choose either story, and retell it in a creative format.

Lesson Ten

Introduction

In the last lesson, we saw examples of Fabius' wisdom in guiding and correcting those under his authority. This passage again shows his understanding of human nature, but then leads into something bigger: the regaining of the town of Tarentum.

Vocabulary

abstained from visiting: did not visit

garrison: military post, fortified area

mercenary: fighting only for pay

scenting the design: sniffing out the plot

incontinently: immediately

furlong: A Roman furlong was 625 feet, or 190.5 m.

Historic Occasions

212 B.C.: Tarentum occupied by Hannibal

211 B.C.: Scipio's father and uncle were killed fighting Hannibal's brother Hasdrubal Barca in Spain; Scipio was made proconsul (governor) of Spain, and defeated Hasdrubal's army in 209 B.C.

209 B.C.: Fabius recaptured Tarentum

On the Map

Tarentum: seaport city in Italy, now called Taranto. Taranto gave its name to both the tarantula and the tarantella.

Bruttians: a tribe of southern Italy

Rhegium: now called Reggio di Calabria

Caulonia: a municipality in Calabria

Reading

Moreover, Fabius after such a sort, recovered again the city of **Tarentum**, and brought it to the obedience of the Romans, which they had lost by treason.

It fortuned there was a young man in his camp, a Tarentine born, that had a sister within Tarentum, which was very faithful to him, and loved him marvellous dearly. Now there was a captain, a **Bruttian** born, that fell in love with her, and was one of those to whom Hannibal had committed the charge of the city of Tarentum. This gave the young soldier, the Tarentine, very good hope, and a way to bring his enterprise to good effect: whereupon he revealed his intent to Fabius, and (seemingly) fled from his camp, and got into the city of Tarentum, giving it out in the city that he would altogether dwell with his sister.

Now for a few days at his first coming, the Bruttian captain **abstained from visiting**, at the request of the maid his sister, who thought her brother had not known of her love; and shortly after, the young fellow took his sister aside, and said unto her:

> "My good sister, there was a great speech in the Roman camp, that thou wert kept by one of the chiefest captains of the **garrison**: I pray thee if it be so, let me know what he is. For so he be a good fellow, and an honest man (as they say he is) I care not: for wars that turneth all things topsy-turvy, regardeth not of what place or calling he is of, and still maketh virtue of necessity, without respect of shame. And it is a special good fortune, at such time as neither right nor reason rules, to happen yet into

the hands of a good and gracious lord."

His sister, hearing him speak these words, sent for the Bruttian captain to bring him acquainted with her brother, who liked well of both their loves, and endeavoured himself to frame his sister's love in better sort towards him, than it was before: by reason whereof, the captain also began to trust him very much. So at last our Tarentine thought this Bruttian officer well enough prepared to receive the offers he had to make him, and that it would be easy for a **mercenary** man, who was in love, to accept, upon the terms proposed, the large rewards promised by Fabius. In conclusion, the bargain was struck, and the promise made of delivering the town.

[omission for content]

Whilst these matters were thus in process, to draw off Hannibal from **scenting the design**, Fabius sent orders to the garrison in **Rhegium**, that they should waste and spoil the Bruttian country, and should also lay siege to **Caulonia**, and storm the place with all their might. These Rhegian soldiers were about the number of eight thousand, and the most of them traitors, and renegades, from one camp to another; and the worst sort of them, and most defamed of life, were those that Marcellus brought thither out of Sicily; so that in losing them all, the loss were nothing to the commonwealth, and the sorrow much less. So Fabius thought, that putting these fellows out for a prey to Hannibal (as a bait to draw him from those quarters) he should pluck him by this means from Tarentum: and so it came to pass. For Hannibal **incontinently** went thence with his army to entrap them: and in the meantime Fabius went to lay siege to Tarentum.

He had not lain six days before it, but the young man (who together with his sister had drawn the Bruttian captain to this treason) stole out one night to Fabius, to inform him of all, having taken very good marks of that side of the wall the Bruttian captain had taken charge of, who had promised him to keep it secret, and to suffer them to enter that came to assault that side. Yet Fabius would not ground his hope altogether upon the Bruttians executing this treason, but went himself in person to view the place appointed, howbeit without attempting anything for that time: and in the mean season, he gave a general assault to all parts of the city (as well by sea as by land) with great shouts and cries. Then the Bruttian captain, seeing all the citizens and garrison run to that part, where they perceived the noise to be greatest: made a signal unto Fabius, that now was the time. Fabius then caused scaling ladders to be brought, whereupon himself with his company scaled the walls, and so won the city.

But it appeareth here, that ambition overcame him. For first he commanded they should kill all the Bruttians, because it should not be known he had won the city by treason. But this bloody policy failed him: for he missed not only of the glory he looked for, but most deservedly he had the reproach of cruelty and falsehood. At the taking of this city, a marvellous number of the Tarentines were slain; besides there were sold thirty thousand of the chiefest of them, and all the city was sacked: and of the spoil thereof which was carried to the common treasure at Rome, three thousand talents. It is reported also, that when they did spoil and carry away all other spoils left behind, the recorder of the city asked Fabius what his pleasure was to do with the "gods," meaning the tables, and their images: and to that Fabius answered him: "Let us leave the Tarentines their gods that be angry with them."

This notwithstanding, he carried from thence Hercules' statue, that was of a monstrous bigness, and caused it to be set up in the Capitol; and withal did set up his own image in brass a-horseback by him. But in that act he shewed himself far harder-hearted than Marcellus had done; or to say more truly, thereby he made the world know how much Marcellus' courtesy, clemency, and bounty was to be wondered at: as we have written in his *Life*.

News being brought to Hannibal that Tarentum was besieged, he marched presently with all speed possible to raise the siege: and they say he had almost come in time, for he was within forty **furlongs** of the city when he understood the truth of the taking of it. Then said he out aloud, "Sure the Romans have their Hannibal too: for as we won Tarentum, so have we lost it." But after that, to his friends he said privately (and that was the first time they ever heard him speak it), that he saw long before, and now it appeared plainly, that they could not possibly with this small power keep Italy.

Narration and Discussion

Explain Fabius' strategy for re-capturing the city of Tarentum.

What do you think of Hannibal's reaction? After so much success, why did these events discourage him so much?

For older students: Though Plutarch generally admires Fabius, he admits that Fabius' behaviour at the end of this passage was both uncharacteristic and cruel. Why do you think Fabius acted this way? Is it possible for someone who has once shown so much wisdom and grace to completely "blow it" at another time? Should we continue to admire such a person?

Lesson Eleven

Introduction

Fabius, in this lesson, was honoured with a triumphal parade. At this point, however, Plutarch shifts the focus of the story onto a rising star in Rome: the army commander Cornelius Scipio. Fabius was aging; Scipio was less than 30 years old. Fabius was still holding back in the long-running war with Hannibal; Scipio was ready to take the war into Carthage itself. Fabius was losing the confidence of the people; Scipio was gaining it. Was it time for Fabius to step down?

Vocabulary

foil his arts: defeat his skills

ineffectual: powerless

dissolute: corrupt

citadel: fort

they chose his son consul: Plutarch appears to have his chronology slightly off, as the son of Fabius (Quintus Fabius Maximus) had been consul a few years before this. Or he may simply be referring to the general respect that the Romans held for them.

lighted straight: got off his horse

went a good round pace: hurried

obsequies: rites

protracted: lengthened

impeded the levies: interfered with the drafting of soldiers to go against Hannibal

declaimed: declared publicly

at their gates: "Hannibal at the gates" (see introductory notes for this study)

the legions which were already in Sicily: Sicily was being used as a sort of dumping ground for soldiers who had survived unsuccessful battles, and who were therefore something of an embarrassment. However, these soldiers were well trained, and they were motivated to prove themselves again in battle; so Scipio was able to assemble a very good army.

People

Crassus: Manius Otacilius Crassus, consul in 263 B.C. and 246 B.C. *(not the Crassus from Plutarch's Life of Crassus)*

Cornelius Scipio: see introductory notes for this study

Historic Occasions

213 B.C.: Quintus Fabius Maximus was consul; Cornelius Scipio was aedile. (Scipio was technically not old enough but was elected anyway.)

206 B.C.: Scipio defeated the Carthaginian forces in Spain and returned to Rome

205 B.C.: Scipio was consul. His plan to take a large military force to Africa was resisted, and he was limited to existing troops in Sicily.

Reading

Part One

Upon this success, Fabius had a triumph decreed him at Rome, much more splendid that his first; they looked upon him now as a champion who had learned to cope with his opponent, and could now easily **foil his arts** and prove his best skill **ineffectual**. And, indeed, the army of Hannibal was at this time partly worn away with continual action, and partly weakened and become **dissolute** with overabundance and luxury. Marcus Livius, who was governor of Tarentum when it was betrayed to Hannibal, and then retired into the **citadel**, which he kept till the town was retaken, was annoyed at these honours and distinctions; and, on one occasion, being drowned with envy and ambition, he burst out and said: that it was himself, not Fabius, that was cause of taking of the city of Tarentum again. Fabius smiling to hear him, answered him openly, "Indeed thou sayest true: for if thou hadst not lost it, I had never won it again."

But the Romans in all other respects did greatly honour Fabius, and specially for that **they chose his son consul**. He, having already taken possession of his office, as he was dispatching certain causes touching the wars, his father, either by reason of age and infirmity, or perhaps out of design to try his son, came up to him on horseback. While he was still at a distance, the young consul observed it, and bade one of his lictors command his father to alight, and tell him if he had any business with the consul, he should come on foot. This commandment misliked the people that heard it, and they all looked upon Fabius, but said not a word: thinking with themselves, that the consul did great wrong to his father's greatness. So he **lighted straight**, and **went a good round pace** to embrace his son, and said unto him: "Yes, my son, you do well to show over whom you command, understanding the authority of a consul, which place you have received. This was the way by which we and our forefathers advanced the dignity of Rome, preferring ever her honour and service to our own fathers and children."

[*omission for length*]

But it fortuned that this son of Fabius died before him, whose death he took patiently, like a wise man, and a good father. Now the custom being at that time, that at the death of a nobleman, their nearest kinsman should make a funeral oration in their praise at their **obsequies**: he himself made the same oration in honour of his son, and committed it afterwards in writing.

Part Two

After Cornelius Scipio, who was sent into Spain, had driven the Carthaginians, defeated by him in many battles, out of the country, and had gained over to Rome many towns and nations with large resources, he was received at his coming home with unexampled joy and acclamation of the people, who, to show their gratitude, elected him consul for the year ensuing. Knowing what high expectations they had of him, he thought the occupation of contesting Italy with Hannibal a mere old man's employment, and proposed no less a task to himself than to make Carthage the seat of the war and fill the province of Africa with arms and devastation; and so oblige Hannibal, instead of invading the countries of others, to draw back and defend his own. And to this end he proceeded to exert all the influence he had with the people.

But Fabius contrarily, persuading himself that the enterprise this young rash youth took in hand was utterly to overthrow the commonwealth, or to put the state of Rome in great danger: he devised to put Rome in the greatest fear he could, without sparing speech or deed he thought might serve for his purpose, to make the people change from that mind. Now he could so cunningly work his purpose, what with speaking and doing, that he had drawn all the Senate to his opinion. But the common people judged it was the secret envy he bore to Scipio's glory, and that he was afraid lest this young conqueror should achieve some great and noble exploit, and have the glory, perhaps, of driving Hannibal out of Italy, or even of ending the war, which had for so many years continued and been **protracted** under his management.

For my part, methinks the only matter that moved Fabius from the beginning to be against Scipio, was the great care he had of the safety of the commonwealth, by reason of the great danger depending upon such a resolution. And yet I do think also, that afterwards he went further than he should, contending too sore against him (whether it was through ambition or obstinacy) seeking to hinder and suppress the greatness of Scipio: considering also he did his best to persuade Crassus, Scipio's companion in the consulship, that he should not grant unto him the leading of the army, but if he thought good to go into Africa, to make wars upon the Carthaginians, that he should rather go himself. He also hindered the giving of money to Scipio for the war; so that he was forced to raise it upon his own credit and interest from the cities of Etruria, which were extremely attached to him. On the other side, Crassus would not stir against him, nor remove out of Italy, being, in his own nature, averse to all contention, and also having, by his office of high priest, religious duties to retain him.

Fabius, therefore, tried other ways to oppose the design; he **impeded the levies**, and he **declaimed**, both in the senate and to the people, that Scipio was not only himself fleeing from Hannibal, but was also endeavouring to drain Italy of all its forces, and to spirit away the youth of the country to a foreign war, leaving behind them their parents, wives, and children, and the city itself, a defenseless prey to the conquering and undefeated enemy **at their gates**.

With this he so far alarmed the people, that at last they would only allow Scipio for the war **the legions which were already in Sicily**, and three hundred, whom he particularly trusted, of those men who had served with him in Spain. In these transactions, Fabius seems to have followed the dictates of his own wary temper.

Narration and Discussion

From **Lesson Five:** "Fabius quietly reminded [Minucius] that it was, in all wisdom, Hannibal, and not Fabius, whom he had to combat; but if he must needs contend with his colleague, it had best be in diligence and care for the preservation of Rome…" Had Fabius forgotten these words, or was he still carrying them out? Why did he find it difficult to trust Scipio's vision for overcoming Hannibal?

Creative narration: Imagine (acted out or in writing) a conversation between Fabius and someone trying to convince him that this time—and only this time—he was just plain wrong.

For older students: In his book *Mere Christianity*, C.S. Lewis wrote, "It is a mistake to think that some of our impulses—say mother love or patriotism—are good, and others, like the fighting instinct, are bad…Strictly speaking, there are no such things as good and bad impulses. A piano has not got two kind of notes on it, the "right" notes and the 'wrong" ones. Every single note is right at one time and wrong at another." How did Fabius' patriotism make him an excellent ruler? Was there anything wrong or misplaced about it?

Lesson Twelve and Examination Questions

Introduction

The war against Hannibal was suddenly going much better for Rome, thanks mostly to Cornelius Scipio. Fabius was still highly respected for what he had done over his lifetime, but his opinions on current affairs were no longer taken too seriously (although he did still have some ability to worry people with his pronouncements).

Vocabulary

spoils: riches

alleging: claiming

happy: fortunate

Historic Occasions

203 B.C.: Death of Fabius

183 B.C.: Death of Scipio

149-146 B.C.: Third Punic War, which ended the independent existence of Carthage

Reading

Now Scipio was no sooner arrived in Africa, but news was brought to Rome of wonderful exploits, and noble service done beyond measure, of which the fame was confirmed by the **spoils** he sent home; of a Numidian king taken prisoner; of a vast slaughter of their men; of two camps of the enemy burnt and destroyed; and in them a great quantity of arms and horses; and when, hereupon, the Carthaginians were compelled to send envoys to Hannibal to call him home, and leave his idle hopes in Italy, to defend Carthage. These wonderful great fortunes of Scipio made him of such renown and fame within Rome, that there was no talk of anything but Scipio. Fabius, notwithstanding, insisted that they should send him a successor, **alleging** no other cause nor reason but the old belief that it was a dangerous thing to commit to the fortune of one man alone so great exceeding prosperity and good success, because it is a rare matter to see one man **happy** in all things.

These words were so much misliked by the people, that they thought him an envious and troublesome man; or else they thought his age had made him fearful; or a fear, that had now become exaggerated, of the skill of Hannibal. For now though Hannibal was forced to leave Italy, and to return into Africa, yet Fabius would not grant that the people's joy and security they thought they were in, was altogether clear, and without fear and mistrust: but gave it out that then they were in greatest danger, and that the commonwealth was breeding more mischief now, than before.

> "For when Hannibal" (said he), "shall return home
> into Africa, and come before the walls of Carthage,
> the Romans shall be less able to abide him there,
> than they have been before: and Scipio moreover,
> shall meet with an army yet warm with the blood of
> so many praetors, dictators, and consuls of Rome,
> which they have overcome, and put to the sword in
> Italy."

With these uncomfortable speeches, he still troubled and disquieted the whole city, persuading them that notwithstanding the war was transferred out of Italy into Africa, yet that the occasion of fear was no less near unto Rome, than it was ever before. Scipio, however, shortly afterwards fought Hannibal, and utterly defeated him, humbled the pride of Carthage beneath his feet, gave his countrymen joy and exultation beyond all their hopes, and—

Long shaken on the seas restored the state.

Howbeit Fabius lived not to the end of this war, nor ever heard while he lived the joyful news of Hannibal's happy overthrow; neither were his years prolonged to see the happy assured prosperity of his country: for about that time that Hannibal departed out of Italy, a sickness took him, whereof he died.

The stories declare that the Thebans buried Epaminondas at the common charges of the people: because he died in so great poverty, that when he was dead, they found nothing in the house but a little iron coin. Fabius did not need this, but the people, as a mark of their affection, defrayed the expenses of his funeral by a private contribution from each citizen of the smallest piece of coin; thus owning him their common father, and making his end no less honourable than his life.

Narration and Discussion

Did Scipio owe some of his eventual success over Hannibal to what Fabius had done before him? Explain.

Creative narration: Describe the peoples' attitude toward Fabius as demonstrated by their actions at his death. Imagine a speech that might be given at his funeral. What words would sum up his character, his leadership, and his contribution to Rome?

For older students: If you read Plutarch's *Life of Pericles* last term, you may want to find and read Plutarch's comparison of Pericles and Fabius; or try writing your own. What did they have in common? What were their differences?

Examination Questions

Younger Students:

1. a) Why did the Romans choose Fabius as dictator? b) Tell about a time when Fabius showed kindness to someone under his authority.

2. (Alternative) Why did Minucius call Fabius "Father?"

Older Students:

3. Tell how Fabius handled the Romans during a time of crisis in the city.

4. Hannibal "dreaded Marcellus when he was in motion, and Fabius when he sat still." Explain.

5. (For high school) Compare and contrast the characters of Fabius and Marcellus OR Fabius and Scipio, giving illustrations. OR "And so it was with the Romans; the counsels and actions of Fabius, which, before the battle, they had branded as cowardice and fear; now, in the other extreme, they accounted to have been more than human wisdom…" Explain these words of Plutarch.

Bibliography

Brooke, C.F. Tucker. *Shakespeare's Plutarch: Containing the Main Sources of Julius Caesar.* London: Chatto & Windus, 1909. (Marcus Brutus)

Plutarch's Lives of the Noble Greeks and Romans. Englished by Sir Thomas North. With an introduction by George Wyndham. Second Volume. London: Dent, 1894. (Pericles, Fabius)

Plutarch's Lives: The Dryden Plutarch. Revised by Arthur Hugh Clough, Volume 1. London: J.M. Dent, 1910. (Pericles, Fabius)

Plutarch's Lives: The Dryden Plutarch. Revised by Arthur Hugh Clough, Volume 3. London: J.M. Dent, 1910 (Marcus Brutus)

About the Author

Anne E. White (www.annewrites.ca) has shared her knowledge of Charlotte Mason's methods through magazine columns, online writing, and conference workshops. She is an Advisory member of AmblesideOnline and the author of *Minds More Awake: The Vision of Charlotte Mason*, as well as other books in The Plutarch Project series.

Made in the USA
Monee, IL
05 August 2022

10862850R00105